SURVEYING YACHTS AND SMALL CRAFT

CONTENTS

THE SURVEY INSPECTION IN MANAGEABLE STAGES

Dedication
This book is dedicated to my two wonderful sons, Jono and Simon, without whose constant badgering I would never have completed it.

Acknowledgements
This book grew out of the practical surveying courses I have run at the International Boatbuilding Training College Lowestoft, and those courses would not have been possible without the support of Fox's Marina and Fox's Yacht Sales of Ipswich.

I should also like to thank my good friend William Walsh, surveyor of *Athens*, who first suggested I write this book and refused to let the matter drop till I did.

INTRODUCTION

This book is not a dissertation on the world of yacht and small craft surveying. Nor is it a mere repetition of the various mandatory standards or voluntary codes of practice that apply to these vessels - a few hours online will readily turn up a plethora of information in that respect. No, this is essentially a highly illustrated 'doing' book that grew out of the practical yacht and small craft survey courses I run at the International Boatbuilding Training College Lowestoft, **www.ibtc.co.uk**.

If you are 'going equipped to survey', what do you actually do when you turn up on site? Where do you start? What tools will you need? What sort of defects are you likely to find? What do they look like? How do you quantify them? How do you record the information as you work? How do you write the subsequent survey report? All these questions and more are answered in the following pages.

This book will appeal to those contemplating a career in surveying and perhaps pursuing one of the predominantly theory-based distance learning courses, but will also be invaluable for anyone proposing to buy or sell a second-hand boat. With the help of this book, as a potential buyer you will be able to carry out your own pre-survey inspections and rule out unsound or badly maintained vessels at an early stage. It will also appeal to those boat owners who would like to understand their vessels better and be able to recognise potential defects in a timely manner, perhaps in preparation for placing the vessel on the market. Well prepared boats will always sell ahead of lesser examples.

So what is a small craft surveyor? Above all he is an assessor of condition, and although he may be many other things such as a naval architect, marine engineer, master mariner, boatbuilder, experienced yachtsman, boat owner etc, his primary function is to find defects and subsequently put them into context. His additional experience in related fields will be useful in this process but unless he can detect and quantify defects he will fall at the first hurdle. This book is thus not overly technical, concentrating instead on detecting and understanding defects.

Wherever I refer to he in this book I mean he or she. Surveying has traditionally been a male preserve, however this is changing. At the time of writing 25% of the delegates on the current IBTC training course are women and they are not the first to have completed the course. The collective noun for a group of surveyors is an 'argument'. So I do not claim that the methods described in this book are the only ones worthy of consideration. What I can claim, however, is that the methods described here have enabled me to enjoy a successful career in the field I love.

LIST OF ABBREVIATIONS

ABYC	American Boat and Yacht Council
Ah	Amp-hour rating, the capacity of a battery
BMC	British Motor Corporation
BMSE	British Marine Surveyors Europe
BSEN	British Standard European Norm
BSS	Boat Safety Scheme
CE (marking)	CE marking is a declaration by the manufacturer that the product meets all the appropriate provisions of the relevant legislation, implementing certain European Directives
CORGI	Now the Gas Safe Register, the body for ensuring high standards of gas appliance and installation work
DZR	Dezincification Resistant Brass
FRP	Fibre Reinforced Plastic
GRP	Glass Reinforced Plastic
HCC	Hull Construction Certificate
HIN	Hull Identification Number
IIMS	International Institute of Marine Surveying
IMEST	Institute of Marine Engineering Science and Technology
ISO	International Standards Organisation
LPG	Liquefied Petroleum Gas
MCA	Maritime and Coastguard Agency
PI	Professional Indemnity Insurance
RCD	Recreational Craft Directive
RINA	Royal Institute of Naval Architects
RNLI	Royal National Lifeboat Institution
RYA	Royal Yachting Association
SSR	Small Ships Register
UV	Ultraviolet
VHF	VHF radio
YDSA	Yacht Designers and Surveyors Association

CHAPTER 1: **MANDATORY STANDARDS, SURVEYING BODIES AND TERMINOLOGY**

Before we turn to practical matters it is necessary to take a brief look at the yacht and small craft survey scene and the various bodies involved in it. The following is only a brief outline but extensive additional information is available online.

WHAT STANDARDS APPLY TO THE TYPE OF CRAFT WE ARE MOST LIKELY TO ENCOUNTER?

The following are mandatory:

Recreational Craft Directive (RCD)

This is an EU wide standard. It is a CE marking directive which sets out a uniform level of safety in the design and manufacture of recreational craft throughout the European Economic Area. It covers craft for sporting and recreational purposes with hull lengths between 2.5 and 24 metres as well as certain items of equipment. All recreational vessels placed on the market in the European Economic Area and built 15 June 1998 onwards would normally comply with this legislation, and the penalties for not doing so are severe. The standard also applies to non-compliant craft entering the EU and being placed on the market after the above date. A few vessels are exempt or excluded and we will look at these later in the survey checklist section of the book.

The directive also lays out requirements for type testing and quality control procedures. The protection requirements are dealt with in depth and organised under 30 headings. The directive contains both administrative and protective requirements for recreational craft. The administrative requirements include marking with a CE plate, which defines the category in which the vessel has been placed. These categories set out the maximum wind strength and wave height in which the vessel should be operated, number of persons carried etc and have become a kind of benchmark to express the vessel's capabilities. Every vessel must also have a declaration of conformity and a technical file.

The RCD is a complex piece of legislation and embodies numerous ISO standards. Extensive further information is available via the internet although the full standard itself cannot be obtained without payment.

The RYA is a good starting point for information and there are various specialist companies offering extensive information and downloads on their websites, such as **www.ceproof.com** and **www. conformance.co.uk**. A comprehensive guide to the RCD can also be downloaded at **www.berr.gov.uk/ files/file11294.pdf**.

The categories in which craft are classified are as follows:

CATEGORY	SIGNIFICANT WAVE HEIGHT	BEAUFORT WIND STRENGTH
A - Ocean	Exceeding 4m	Exceeding 8
B - Offshore	Up to and including 4m	Up to and including 8
C - Inshore	Up to and including 2m	Up to and including 6
D - Sheltered	Up to and including 0.3m	Up to and including 4

The Boat Safety Scheme (BSS)

This is a UK wide standard. The BSS was jointly established in 1997 by the Environment Agency and British Waterways to promote safety on the inland waterways in respect of boats, their installations and their components. Meeting these safety standards in order to obtain a navigation licence became a requirement at the same time. Boat Safety Scheme inspections can only be carried out by operatives who have undertaken the BSS training course. Further information is available from **www. boatsafetyscheme.com** including an excellent downloadable manual intended for preparing a craft for inspection. Some of the standards within this BSS manual have been adopted by surveyors assessing other craft not subject to the BSS, and if used sensibly is a very useful document. Schemes apply to both privately owned and non privately owned boats.

Maritime and Coastguard Agency Code of Practice

This code applies to small commercial vessels operating in British waters or under the British flag. All UK vessels in commercial use, up to 24 metres load line length, which go to sea and carry no more than

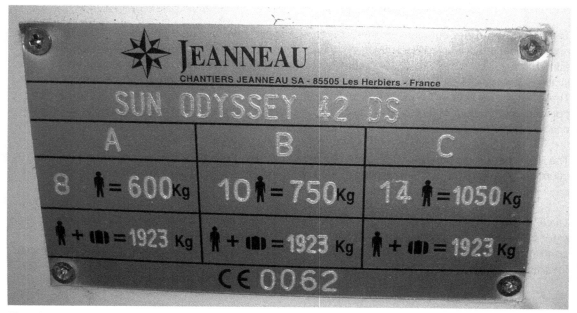

Fig 1: CE Plate on a 2009 Jeanneau Sun Odyssey 42DS yacht. This vessel is classified as 'A (Ocean)', the highest category. She has however also been classified in the lower categories with a heavier payload. This system of marking is universal throughout the EU and the format is laid down in the Directive.

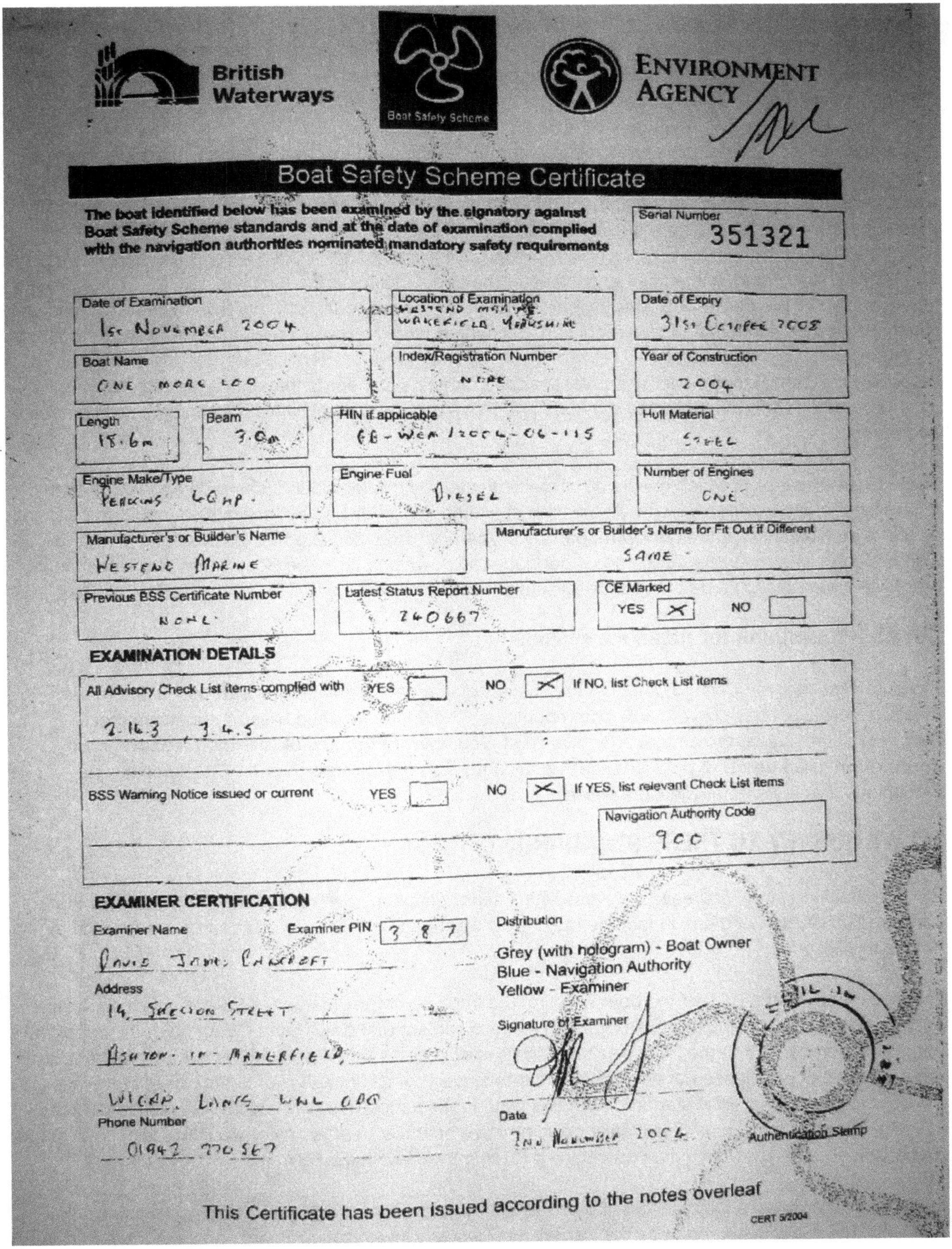

British Waterways

Boat Safety Scheme

ENVIRONMENT AGENCY

Boat Safety Scheme Certificate

The boat identified below has been examined by the signatory against Boat Safety Scheme standards and at the date of examination complied with the navigation authorities nominated mandatory safety requirements

Serial Number 351321

Date of Examination: 1st November 2004	Location of Examination: Westend Marine, Wakefield, Yorkshire	Date of Expiry: 31st October 2008
Boat Name: One More Leo	Index/Registration Number: None	Year of Construction: 2004
Length: 18.6m / Beam: 3.0m	HIN if applicable: GB-WEM 12004-06-115	Hull Material: Steel
Engine Make/Type: Perkins 60hp.	Engine Fuel: Diesel	Number of Engines: One
Manufacturer's or Builder's Name: Westend Marine	Manufacturer's or Builder's Name for Fit Out if Different: Same	
Previous BSS Certificate Number: None.	Latest Status Report Number: 240667	CE Marked: YES [X] NO [ ]

EXAMINATION DETAILS

All Advisory Check List items complied with YES [ ] NO [X] If NO, list Check List items

2.16.3, 3.4.5

BSS Warning Notice issued or current YES [ ] NO [X] If YES, list relevant Check List items

Navigation Authority Code 900

EXAMINER CERTIFICATION

Examiner Name: David James Cancroft

Examiner PIN: 3 8 7

Address: 14, Sheldon Street, Ashton-in-Makerfield, Wigan, Lancs WN4 0DG

Phone Number: 01942 770 567

Distribution
Grey (with hologram) - Boat Owner
Blue - Navigation Authority
Yellow - Examiner

Signature of Examiner

Date: 2nd November 2004

Authentication Stamp

This Certificate has been issued according to the notes overleaf

CERT 5/2004

Fig 2: Boat Safety Scheme Certificate. The certificate should be kept aboard the vessel and available for inspection.

12 passengers and/or cargo, are required by law to comply with the MCA (Maritime and Coastguard Agency) Small Commercial Vessel and Pilot Boat Code of Practice and be issued with certificates by an Authorised Certifying Authority. The number of persons that the vessel carries can be greater than 12, for example 10 crew and 12 passengers.

This legislation also covers pleasure craft in commercial use such as charter yachts, sailing schools, commercial angling and dive boats, and is an extensive code covering all aspects of the vessel's soundness, stability, suitability, equipment and manning. It is a stringent code intended to protect both those operating and paying for a service in craft that proceed to sea.

The MCA appoint various agencies to administer the code, including the RYA and YDSA. Only approved surveyors who have been nominated by one of the agencies may carry out this work, which involves an initial compliance examination plus regular inspections during the 5 year life of the compliance certificate.

Much like the Boat Safety Scheme above, the code contains standards that surveyors refer to when assessing other craft not subject to the code and if this is done sensibly it is again a very useful source of information.

The Harmonised Code, which covers all vessels affected by this legislation, can be downloaded from the MCA website, **www.mcga.gov.uk**. At the time of writing it is in full use but not ratified, and can be found as a Marine Guidance Note at **www.mcga.gov.uk/c4mca/mgn_280-2.pdf**. Much useful information can also be found at **www.ydsa.co.uk**. It is a good idea to download both the Boat Safety Scheme manual and MCA Harmonised Code of Practice for future reference.

SOLAS Regulations for pleasure vessels

Pleasure vessels over 45 ft (13.7m) LOA are subject to stringent regulation for safety equipment etc. Pleasure vessels of this size are now commonplace but owners are often blissfully unaware that their vessels are subject to a mandatory standard. See **www.mcga.gov.uk/c4mca/pleasure_craft_ information_packdec07-2.pdf**. This site has full details and also refers to SOLAS V, some simple regulations that apply to all pleasure vessels.

DO WE SURVEY TO THESE STANDARDS?

If you are looking at coastal/seagoing vessels in use for pleasure, it will be immediately apparent that a very large proportion of them, in fact the majority, will not be subject to any mandatory standard at all. Why is this?

If we look firstly at the RCD, if the boat was first put into use before 15 June 1998 and was in EEA waters on that date, she is completely exempt. Even if she is subject to the RCD and CE marked, the important thing to remember is that the RCD dies once the vessel is first sold. At present there is no mechanism to regularly check compliance nor any requirement to stay in compliance. It is of course possible to assess the boat to the original RCD standards but this would take a month or two and involve dismantling the vessel amongst other things. It is clearly good practice however to note any obvious modifications made to the vessel since she was built, particularly if these may affect essential items.

In 2005, the *Megawat*, a four year old Hanse sailing yacht, lost her rudder and sank in 40 minutes in the Irish Sea. The subsequent report by the Irish Marine Casualty Investigation Board concluded that the fitting of an autopilot subsequent to her being sold new had contributed to the loss. As part of the investigation the European Commission suggested that where modifications of essential parts had been made the vessel should be treated as new and re-assessed. Ostensibly this placed an impossibly heavy burden on surveyors inspecting second-hand RCD compliant vessels in the normal course of their business, for example a pre-purchase survey, but at the time of writing this principle has not been implemented. The full *Megawat* report, including the comments from the European Commission, can be downloaded from **www. ncib.ie** and it makes very interesting reading.

Obviously these coastal and seagoing craft will not be covered by the Boat Safety Scheme, although a few motor yachts that spend some time inland, on the Thames or Norfolk Broads for example, will be certificated. Any coastal/seagoing vessels in commercial use and proceeding to sea will of course (or should!) be certificated under the MCA Code of Practice. Unfortunately, however, this is not quite what it seems. If vessels operate exclusively in what are termed Categorised Waters they are deemed not to go to sea and there is no requirement for them to comply with the Code of Practice. Some of these waters are considered to be amongst the most hazardous around the British coast, for example the sandbank-ridden Thames Estuary – a very dangerous place for a small vessel in bad weather.

IF WE ARE NOT SURVEYING TO ANY PARTICULAR COMMON STANDARD, WHERE DO WE START?

Firstly the majority of boat owners will not consider it reasonable for a surveyor to impose a set of standards on his or her vessel if those standards do not apply to that vessel, and this is a perfectly reasonable attitude. Equally the boat owner or potential owner in a pre-purchase scenario will want to know that the boat is sound and safe.

So in the absence of any set standard the surveyor takes on the weighty responsibility of creating a format that fulfils the client's requirement and that of others who may reasonably be expected to rely on the survey, typically insurance companies and finance houses (but not Tom, Dick or Harry who subsequently buys the boat on the strength of an existing survey report). This also defines the parties a surveyor is liable to in the event of a dispute. It thus follows that a good starting point are the criteria that insurance companies specify should be covered in an Insurance survey which they require their insured client to provide.

Next we will look at the Codes of Practice published by the various bodies involved in surveying, to which their surveyor members are required to comply. These can usually be found on the appropriate websites.

The pre-purchase survey format used in this book is an amalgam of the above plus other criteria, some of which are based on standards contained in both the MCA Code of Practice and the Boat Safety Scheme. Other useful sources of information are the *RYA Boat Safety Handbook*, publication C8, **www. rya.org.uk/shop/products/Pages/c8.aspx** and the *RNLI Seacheck Scheme*, **www.rnli.org.uk**.

Constructing a format that is fit for purpose is a considerable responsibility. The one used in this book has found favour with all interested parties and is one that I have successfully used over many years. It is, however, just one format amongst many that are equally successful and valid.

The scope of this book is confined to standard FRP production boats; other formats would be used for specialist and one-off craft.

Fig 3: The author (left) and fellow surveyor Roger Bell offering different opinions, a common scenario in the survey process.

● WHO REGULATES THIS INDUSTRY?

Actually nobody. Leaving aside the mandatory surveys and inspections described above, there are absolutely no controls and you can set up in business as a general yacht and small craft surveyor tomorrow if you like. You do not even have to take out Professional Indemnity (PI) Insurance but you would be very foolish not to. Having said that, there are numerous surveyors working without PI either because they resent paying the premium or they have had so many claims against them as to be uninsurable. I know of one guy who was a carpet fitter one week and a 'surveyor' the next but his new career was a short one.

ASSOCIATIONS, INSTITUTES AND PROFESSIONAL BODIES OPERATING IN THE FIELD

In reality of course the vast majority of surveyors belong to one or more of these groupings and are bound by their rules and standards. However, the criteria for membership varies across the groups and some are more weighted towards commercial shipping. The majority of UK surveyors will belong to one or more of the following:

The Yacht Designers and Surveyors Association (YDSA) is widely acknowledged to be at the forefront of yacht and small craft surveying. It sets very high membership criteria and amongst its members you will find surveyors able to undertake every aspect of the work. Visit **www.ydsa.co.uk**.

British Marine Surveyors Europe (BMSE) was established in 2007 but has rapidly established itself as a respected group. Membership is restricted to graduates of the IBTC practical surveying course and it is a condition of membership that surveyors share technical experience, articles etc via the BMSE private forums and wiki, which has become a most valuable technical resource. Visit **www.bmse.co.uk**.

The Royal Institute of Naval Architects (RINA) is a world respected Institute with highly qualified members with diverse expertise across the whole maritime sector, including yachts and small craft. Visit **www.rina.org.uk**.

The International Institute of Marine Surveying (IIMS) is an international organisation involved in commercial shipping but with a small craft group. Visit **www.iims.org.uk**.

Institute of Marine Engineering Science and Technology (IMEST) is an international organisation primarily involved in commercial shipping but with a small craft group. Visit **www.imarest.org**.

TERMINOLOGY YOU WILL COME ACROSS IN THE DESCRIPTION OF PLEASURE CRAFT

A good deal of confusion exists as to the tonnage, weight and registration of pleasure craft. Below are the commonly used terms plus a short definition.

1. **Registered Tonnage:** This is a measurement of internal volume derived from the number of 'tuns' or barrels of wine a merchant ship could carry. It is found by taking a few measurements and calculating a nominal internal volume using a simple formula, and is a mandatory part of full British registration as defined below. Please note where a registration has lapsed a new tonnage measurement will still have to be carried out even if the original figures are available.

2. **Thames Tonnage:** This is an obsolete term which applied to pleasure vessels only and is again based on a measurement of internal volume, but for any given vessel the figure will be significantly different to the registered tonnage described above and there is no correlation between the two figures. It was introduced by the Royal Thames Yacht Club in 1854 and amended in 1962. You will still find many older wooden yachts referred to by their Thames Tonnage and many builders identified their standard designs by their Thames Tonnage, hence Hillyard 12 tonner, Yachting World 5 tonner etc. It is never used for modern yachts and usually only means anything to yachtsmen of a certain age.

3. **Racing Rules:** There used to be a system for classifying racing boats, from quarter tonners about 25ft long like the *Robber*, up to 2 tonners as used in the Admiral's Cup. This has nothing to do with internal volume or weight but most yachtsmen of middle age would know what was meant by a half or threequarter tonner, for example.

4. **Full British Registration, aka Part One Registration:** This is the highest form of registration available to pleasure craft and is very similar to that for a commercial ship. It used to

guarantee absolute proof of title but that is no longer the case, although it is as close as you can get. Because ships were often owned by syndicates the title is divided into 64 shares and with yachts these are often divided between husband and wife. If a finance house is lending money for a boat purchase they will normally insist the vessel be Part One registered and the loan or mortgage will be registered against the ship with the Registrar of British Ships in Cardiff. Anyone can obtain, for a fee, a transcript of the registration to check this. When a vessel is being sold, the phrase 'free of all encumbrances' will be seen on the bill of sale and this is a declaration by the owner(s) that no mortgages or other unpaid debts attach to the vessel. All Part One registered vessels will carry an official number, seen on board as 'Off No 123456,' plus her registered tonnage derived from the tonnage measurement. Details at: **www.mcga.gov.uk/c4mca/ukr-home/pleasurecraft-smallships.htm**.

5. **Small Ships Register, aka Part Three Registration:** This was introduced about 30 years ago as a simpler and less expensive form of registration for pleasure craft. Its sole purpose is to identify the vessel as British when cruising abroad and for any other purpose it is not worth the paper it is printed on. It most certainly does not infer any proof of title and is very easy to obtain; this can all be done by the owner online at the above site. The vessel will have a number, seen on board with the prefix SSR.

6. **Registered at Lloyds or 'Lloyds Registered':** These terms crop up with older boats and simply mean that the vessel was included in the very long established but now defunct Lloyds Register of Yachts. In days gone by most larger yachts would, upon payment of a fee, be listed in this publication. From memory it was only yachts over 4 tons Thames measurement that could be included. In real terms this 'registration' means very little, and most importantly nothing in terms of proof of title. The register carried on into the 1980s so these terms are still encountered on a regular basis.

7. **Weight:** None of the above tonnages or registration have anything whatsoever to do with the total weight of the vessel, which of course is also the displacement. Many owners however think registered tonnage is the weight. Most RCD compliant boats will have the 'lightship', or unladen weight, recorded in the mandatory owner's manual, plus a laden weight with tanks full and maximum complement aboard as defined on the CE plate. This latter weight is sometimes required when coding the vessel. Note weight, or displacement, will be found expressed in tons, tonnes or kilograms.

CHAPTER 2: **GOING EQUIPPED TO SURVEY**

WHAT TOOLS WILL WE NEED?

Each surveyor's toolbag will contain a unique and sometimes idiosyncratic collection of tools. There are of course many standard items but surveyors often find the most unexpected use for a common tool in the survey process. Below is a standard list and we will return to their uses in more detail in the practical sections.

1. **Adjustable spanner**
2. **Batteries** – spare for everything and of rechargeable type
3. **Blocks, plywood pads and crowbar** – for aggressively testing deck fittings etc
4. **Chalk** – for marking various defects on hulls etc. Remember to have different colours – many hulls will be white. Please do not use wax crayon for recording moisture readings on hulls being dried down for osmosis treatment – the last thing the yard wants are residual traces of wax left on the substrate
5. **Chisels** – various for digging out mastic etc
6. **Digital camera** – one of the most important tools because it can go where you cannot. Video inspection scopes are also now becoming affordable and a few marine surveyors are using them to great effect
7. **Matchbox** – for providing scale in photos, plus 'Blue-Tack' for attaching it to the object in shot
8. **Digital spirit level** – mainly used in MCA coding
9. **Electrical test meter** – basic model OK
10. **Electrical socket tester (mains)** – for basic checks on shorepower installations
11. **Files various** – for cleaning up metal surfaces for inspection
12. **Feeler gauges** – for forcing into and measuring gaps
13. **Hammers** – small pin hammer for sounding hulls, something larger for various testing
14. **Indicator strips** – for PH testing of blisters
15. **Absorbent cloth/material** – eg kitchen roll, for drying surfaces
16. **Magnet** – for basic testing stainless steel - lower non marine grades are magnetic. Note specialist alloys such as 'Aquamet' used for propeller shafts are magnetic, but these will not be commonly found in production boats
17. **Magnifying glass** – mainly used for finding stress cracks in rigging components etc
18. **Moisture meters**
19. **Measuring tape** – the longer the better
20. **Plumb line** – for marking off measurements to the ground etc mainly in tonnage measurement
21. **Pliers** – general gripping
22. **Powerful rechargeable spotlight** – and carry a spare
23. **Mirrors** – various including extending type
24. **Mole grips** – general gripping
25. **Punches** – various sizes for testing fastenings etc
26. **Rigtester** – electronic (see **www.maidsure.org.uk**)
27. **Scrapers** – tungsten bladed type best. Numerous uses but primarily used to remove patches of antifouling to examine the underlying surface and for taking moisture readings
28. **Something to lie on**

We must pause here and think very seriously. If you pursue a surveying career you will be scraping antifouling most working days of your life so it is paramount to protect your lungs from antifouling dust. The compositions in antifouling are constantly changing and there is a real risk that serious health problems could come to light in the longer term where the dust has been inhaled over a long period. So we must wear a mask when undertaking this part of the job.

I go a stage further and use a vacuum scraper connected to a 12v rechargeable vacuum cleaner; this ensures that the tiny particles you can't see are mopped up.

Fig 4: Scraper and 12v vacuum cleaner.

29. **Screwdrivers**
30. **Stiff blade** – for forcing into gaps, ie under mastic at keel/hull joints

The scraper shown above is available from **www.gelplane.co.uk** and the vacuum cleaner came from Argos for a few pounds – money well spent.

31. **Spikes** – various
32. **Straight edge** – for bridging across an area of deflection to measure degree. A simple wooden batten is normally sufficient
33. **Vernier gauge** – for measuring rigging and shaft diameters etc
33. **Wire brush**
35. **A good notebook** – with waterproof cover will be required if you are not going to use the next item

When you are carrying out the survey you will constantly be looking at items then returning to them later during the process, i.e. looking at through hull fittings below the waterline during the external inspection then looking at the associated valves inside the boat perhaps some hours later. So you need the facility to store information in easily accessible folders (or sections if you use a notepad) and be able to scroll back and add to (not overwrite) those folders throughout the survey inspection. If the folder numbers correspond to the numbered sections in your report then you can subsequently write this in a logical manner starting at section one and retrieving all the information from each folder as you proceed in chronological order. Being methodical is essential in this job, and anything that works for you in this respect is to be encouraged and developed.

Recording information

There is one more tool we require and this deserves a section of its own. However good a surveyor is, if he or she cannot record the information methodically and efficiently during the survey inspection a good report will never be produced. So recording information is paramount and requires good organisation. The traditional method is a pen and notebook, with separate sections for each area being inspected. Many surveyors manage with this but I find it particularly awkward in wet and windy weather so I use a small digital voice recorder, an Olympus VN-240. At the time of writing this is a current model, see **www.olympus.co.uk/consumer/2581_VN-240.htm**.

Fig 5: Olympus VN-240 Digital Voice Recorder.
These little devices fit easily into the hand and pocket and are very convenient to use. On the screen we can see that we are in section 13 of the survey (Seacocks, Valves and other Through Hull Fitting and seven separate recordings have already been made in this section. When we get to section 13, writing the report, all information regarding these items is conveniently stored together even though several hours may have separated the recordings during the actual survey inspection.

NOW WE HAVE OUR TOOL KIT AND WE KNOW HOW TO RECORD INFORMATION, WHAT NEXT?

Before we launch into the practical sections we must first briefly fast forward to the report writing aspect of the process because the basic principles of report writing as advocated in this book have a significant bearing on our approach to the survey inspection. We will of course return to building the report format and report writing in more detail in the final chapter.

WHAT ARE WE TRYING TO ACHIEVE IN THE REPORT?

Certainly not what many reports contain, ie a general description of the vessel and multiple disclaimers to cover the surveyor's back. However, most reports contain two distinct streams:

- **Fact: Incontrovertible information about the vessel, ie the main shroud rigging attachment points consist of stainless steel U-bolts through the deck with tie rods under.**

- **Opinion: The main shroud rigging attachment points consisting of stainless steel U-bolts through the deck appeared in good condition.**

What distinguishes a good surveyor from one who is merely competent is the devising and implementing of as many tests as possible in order to move opinion closer to fact, and those tests of course are carried out at the inspection stage.

Let's look at the inspection of the main shroud rigging attachment points in more detail and examine the inspections and tests that would be appropriate, with a view to moving opinion to fact. Here is a list of checks one might make on a typical 35' sailing yacht:

- Check for any obvious movement, distorting to deck, stress cracks in fitting etc. Where U-bolts are used it is important that the bolts are following the rigging attached to them in a nice fair line, otherwise excess stress is placed on the fitting. One often sees vertical U-bolts with lower shrouds attached at an unfair angle.
- Access is often very restricted or impossible from inside the boat. Where this is the case use a moisture meter on linings etc, looking for seepage. If this has been present, long term crevice corrosion may be present in the hidden stainless steel components. Recommend dismantling for full inspection.
- Are the external fittings lying tight and fair to deck? If seepage is present and they are bolted to bulkheads these may also be rotten, particularly behind GRP bonding. Hammer sound and spike test (but no spiking in areas where appearance is important).
- When heavy brown staining to the fixing nuts etc is present crevice, corrosion is probably developing in the threads. The shanks of U-bolts are also very vulnerable where they pass through the deck.
- Where arrangements are in place to dissipate the stresses into other parts of the structure, ie tie rods or plates attached to knees etc bonded into the topsides, check the topsides and adjacent structure externally for distortion. It is essential to state in all reports in this section whether the rig was set up hard or not (or obviously if mast is unstepped). If the rigging is slack, defects may become apparent when it is set up.
- Is the forestay fitting merely bolted to the deck or does it have a plate running down the stem or similar to transfer some of the loadings into the hull? Check all welds for stress cracks.

FUNDAMENTAL REPORT WRITING PRINCIPLE NUMBER ONE
Never confuse fact and opinion.

- If the rigging has been slacked off prior to survey, ask yourself why and aggressively swig the shrouds etc.

All these tests and inspections reinforce your opinion that the component is sound and secure. However, we can go a stage further:

- Test on deck with a 1 metre crowbar using a hardwood block as a pivot placed on a large plywood pad to avoid damage to deck. Get as much leverage as possible and be brutal.

This establishes as an incontrovertible fact that the component withstood such a test without movement or failure and reinforces the overall comment expressed about the component still further, moving it away from opinion and towards fact.

Of course it is essential that every inspection and test carried out is recorded in the report together with their results. This establishes beyond any doubt that they were carried out and explains why you arrived at the conclusions etc stated. It is also vital that the limitations of the test are clearly defined in the report and that the test is appropriate for the size and scale of the component.

When I (failed) to learn algebra at school it was drummed into me to always show my working, and that principle holds good here.

Of course the tests must really add something, be meaningful and appropriate for the type of vessel. My favourite example of this is the oft seen statement: 'the masthead was examined by binocular and all appears in satisfactory condition.' One would be looking for stress cracks in stainless fittings, missing or damaged split pins etc and these would not be detectable from deck level. However, the client will be lulled into a false sense of security by this statement, which is basically a third stream occasionally lamentably found in some survey reports, ie fiction.

In the above illustration you will note that the various tests and inspections carried out have been reduced to a checklist form, and that will continue to be the case throughout the practical sections of the book as we look at the various defects likely to be encountered and their detection.

Fig 6: Where it all starts. Foam stringers being fitted into a hull moulding, ready for over laminating.

CHAPTER 3: **BASIC FRP CONSTRUCTION AND COMMON DEFECTS**

In this chapter we will look at the following:

1. **The material.**
2. **Hull building methods most commonly found in FRP production small craft.**
3. **Deck and superstructure building methods most commonly found in FRP production small craft.**
4. **Ballast keels and associated reinforcing.**

This chapter is not intended as a comprehensive dissertation on FRP boat building or resin chemistry but is a basic overview as to how production FRP yachts and small craft are built, and the most common defects one is likely to encounter. It is written in plain English and every attempt is made to demystify the subject in order that it can be understood by as many people as possible. The information contained therein has been gleaned over many years building, surveying and operating FRP vessels, and the observations made are thus based on experience not just theoretical possibility.

1. THE MATERIAL

GRP, or to be more precise FRP, has been used in production boatbuilding since the late 1950s. GRP (glass reinforced plastic), fibreglass and glassfibre all describe the same basic material – polyester resin reinforced with a variety of glass strands bound together to form some type of glass 'cloth'. This matrix is impregnated with resin which, when cured, forms a strong and stable material. Other forms of reinforcing such as Kevlar and carbon fibre are being used increasingly in conjunction with the basic glass strands due to their enhanced strength to weight characteristics, hence FRP (fibre reinforced plastic) is the correct description. However GRP is still the most widely used description amongst the boating public.

Sandwich construction, whereby an end grain balsa wood or foam core are sandwiched between an inner and outer layer of solid FRP, is also very common, providing great panel stiffness with light weight. Various modified polyester, vinylester and epoxy resins are increasingly seen in production boatbuilding and are common in one off and racing designs.

Production hulls, decks and superstructures are moulded in a female mould and the basic process is very simple. First, the gelcoat (which is just pigmented resin) is painted on the pre-prepared mould surface and allowed to partly harden. Successive layers of glass and resin are then laid on top of this till the required thickness is reached. The moulding is then left till it has cured sufficiently to allow the whole thing to be released and removed from the mould without distorting. It's as simple as that. However, there is one fundamental difference with FRP when compared to wood and steel construction. With the latter two materials one can pre-select the quality of wood or steel used and the rest is down to how good the construction is. The quality of the construction can also be seen and assessed after the vessel has been built.

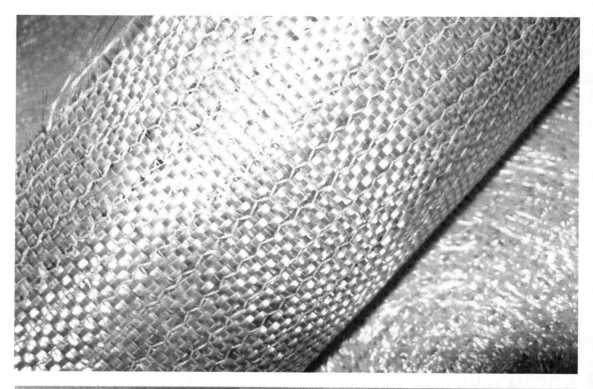

Figs 7&8: The basic glass reinforcing material comes in a huge number of different permutations and often, as can be seen here, consists of two differing types stitched together in one sheet.

Fig 9: End grain balsa squares bonded to a flexible carrier to form a continuous sheet able to take up some curvature in use.

Fig 10: Foam cores pre-cut for use in foam cored stringers (as being fitted in Fig 6).

With FRP the material itself is created from its constituent parts as the boat is moulded. So however good the constituent parts are, the quality of the final material is entirely dependent on the skill and mood of the laminator and quality controllers on the day. Human nature being what it is, this introduces huge and unpredictable variables before the boat is even completed and, unlike wood and steel, once the moulding is finished its quality cannot readily be gauged. Surveyors are constantly finding the results of these variables several years later when they manifest themselves as defects which can be traced right back to the moulding day.

Moulding methods have become increasingly sophisticated in recent years, incorporating automated resin infusion and induction moulding techniques etc largely in response to environmental and health and safety issues, and this has resulted in more consistency although plenty of other problems have emerged to keep surveyors busy. Resin is an oilbased product and cost is also a major driving force to improve resin distribution through the matrix and so reduce the resin to fibre ratio.

So from day one it is important to be aware just how this material is created as the boat is moulded, and of the potential for substantial variation in moulding quality.

2. HULL BUILDING METHODS MOST COMMONLY FOUND IN FRP PRODUCTION SMALL CRAFT

In its simplest form the hull deck structure will be solid FRP (as opposed to sandwich construction) and of sufficient thickness so that little further reinforcing is necessary, this usually provided by various bulkheads and partitions forming the vessel's accommodation. This is commonly seen in older FRP yachts but such a form of construction is both heavy and costly due to the sheer amount of materials necessary to provide sufficient strength and panel stiffness.

At the other end of the production scale are vessels utilising a very light shell moulding stiffened by various frames and longitudinals either incorporated into the shell moulding or as part of an additional inner moulding bonded to the hull shell. These types of construction are much lighter and cheaper to produce. In the quest for accommodation, performance and low price the weight (ie quantity of materials used) is being ever driven downwards and this in conjunction with ever spiralling resin prices means surveyors will continue to be fully occupied in years to come despite improvements in design and technology.

So let's take a look at the various forms of construction, starting with the simplest.

Heavy solid FRP layup, typically consisting of chopped strand matt alone or in conjunction with woven rovings

Back in the early days of FRP boatbuilding its strengths and weaknesses were not well understood and of course resin was relatively cheap. So general construction tended to be simple and heavy: if in doubt, make it thicker. Many vessels from this era survive in good structural condition despite their age and in some cases hard use. One can think of the Nelson series of motor launches used for many years in the pilot service and numerous other commercial applications. In the leisure sector one has the Snapdragons, Westerlies, Nicholsons, Rivals etc and in Holland the Contest range, first moulded in 1959 and still going strong. In common with all others these hulls will suffer the vagaries of moisture absorption to a varying degree but few other serious or even terminal defects, and this after many years very hard use in some cases. The mouldings are simply thick enough so as to flex very little and although the cosmetic condition will deteriorate the structural condition remains sound.

What defects are we likely to encounter with this type of construction, leaving aside those related to moisture ingress to the hull laminate, which we will be returning to later in this chapter?

- **Delamination** where one or more of the layers parts company with its neighbour. This is usually due to poor moulding quality in the first place.
- **Voids and dry areas in the laminate** can again be traced back to the day of moulding but may have remained undetected for many years. Eventually the void will take up moisture, possibly leading to delamination in the surrounding laminate, sometimes referred to as an interlaminar blister. Whatever caused it this is a very serious defect.

Fig 11 shows a section through a hull laminate that has started to delaminate, in this case the result of only a light collision. The delamination is occurring at a junction between layers of chopped strand matt reinforcing and woven roving cloth. This is quite common and usually due to dry areas where the cloth has not been properly saturated with resin (known as 'wetting out').

Fig 12 shows the failed laminate prised apart and it is immediately apparent that resin starvation (or insufficient wetting out) has caused the failure. From the day this moulding was laminated it was bound to fail sooner or later and it is a good illustration of how the quality of the finished material is only as good as the laminator or quality controller on the day.

Delamination and dry areas are detected by light sounding of the hull with a small pin hammer or similar instrument. It is necessary to lightly sound the entire hull, listening for any dead and hollow sounding areas. You will hear changes in tone where bulkheads and other reinforcing members are fitted but this is

Fig 11: Section through delaminating laminate.

Fig 12: Dry area in a laminate leading to delamination.

a quite different sound to the dull hollow sound of delamination. If you come across an FRP hull with very large blisters visible, say 50mm in diameter, then take the opportunity to go over these blisters with your hammer because the hollow sound will be very similar to that heard when delamination is present. Other materials that pass from hollow to solid will produce a very similar effect and it is suggested you take a walk round your home lightly tapping furniture etc to get a feel for this vital test. This will also encourage a light, non destructive touch. In fact only very light tapping is necessary and great care must be taken to use a clean hammer above the waterline on the shiny topsides.

Note that plastic hammers and those faced with resilient material as sometimes recommended elsewhere are not suitable for this test because an additional indicator, which comes with experience, is the degree of 'bounce back' from the hammer and any resilient facing cushions this out.

Fig 13 shows another example of poor wetting out seen from inside the boat. The laminate has been finished with unidirectional glass rovings which can literally be pulled out of the laminate under the bilge paint.

The glass has clearly never seen any resin and we can only guess at the quality of the rest of the moulding. If I were a gambling man, however, I know where my money would be.

Fig 13: Poor wetting out of laminate.

a) **Gelcoat cracking**

Craft with this type of construction will most likely be old and the gelcoat will thus be ageing. This coupled with its thickness, which tends to be excessive, may cause cracking to the surface which will allow moisture ingress. If this has occurred over a long period the laminate may be damaged, but more of this later.

b) **Failure of bonding at bulkheads etc**

As described above the main reinforcing over and above the hull thickness itself will consist of various bulkheads and partitions bonded into the hull. The integrity of that bonding is important and will frequently be found peeling off the plywood bulkhead around the perimeter where it is bonded into the hull. Which leads us into the next common problem.

c) **Rotting plywood bulkheads and partitions**

The FRP laminate may be enjoying a long life but the plywood may not. This is a separate material and its longevity will to a large extent depend on its quality in the first place. Be especially wary if the ply has been wet over a long period, ie in the bilge or where a deck leak has occurred over a long period. Look closely around the edge of the bonding because if moisture has permeated the ply behind the FRP bonding it will never dry out and eventual rot is inevitable.

In this most simple form FRP is at its most reliable and predictable and this is largely due to the lack of flexing within the structure. Any other (non moisture related) defects other than as described above will normally be obvious in the form of wear and tear and damage.

Solid FRP layup with additional reinforcing integral with the shell moulding

This form of construction can suffer from all the defects mentioned above plus the following:

a) The function of the plywood bulkheads and partitions becomes of more structural importance if the shell laminate is generally thinner. Thus any deterioration to the plywood and bonding becomes more significant to the structural integrity.

b) Fracturing and de-bonding of frames and stringers. These are typically of top hat section formed over foam cores or deep web type formed over plywood of about 25mm thickness. It is thus important to decide from the outset whether the plywood or foam core is simply a former for the FRP frame or part of the structure. Plywood webs are often just bonded in place and lightly FRP encapsulated, particularly across keel roots, and any deterioration is clearly a structural defect. An idea of the thickness and type of construction of these webs etc can often be gained where limber holes or accesses for hoses etc have been drilled through and the raw edge can be seen. These should always be sealed with resin but often are not. Obviously those in the highly stressed areas are most prone to deterioration, ie across the keel root where a ballast keel is fitted and where mast compression is concentrated. Fracturing is also commonly found where longitudinal and athwartships members intersect.

c) Flexing and associated gelcoat crazing and laminate fracturing. If, as is likely, the shell is thinner then there is the potential for flexing anywhere in the hull with consequent cracking or crazing of the gelcoat and/or epoxy coatings, plus fracturing of the actual laminate in more severe cases.

Flexing is also likely anywhere that some form of internal stiffening creates a hard spot in the hull. At this point the hull is fully supported and entirely rigid, whereas the adjacent shell is not, so flexing will occur

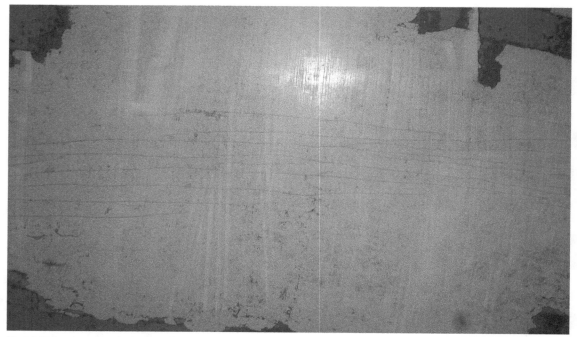

Fig 14: Gelcoat crazing at a hard spot.

either side of the rigid spot, this sometimes referred to as the hinge effect. This is commonly seen in sailing yachts around bulkheads and other partitions.

In Fig 14, the gelcoat crazing running longitudinally is where the hull has flexed in the forward sections above and below a hard spot where a forward berth is bonded into the hull and is typical of the defect. Such cracks and crazing as this are often visible through antifouling when a vessel has just been brought ashore and the antifouling surface has dried off. However, the underlying cracks retain the moisture and can often be seen as clear lines on the otherwise dry antifouling surface. This is very useful when the surveyor is present during the lift.

How do we know whether this is mere crazing of the gelcoat or cracks that extend into the laminate, a serious defect?

The short answer is that we don't and it is very difficult indeed to tell. Some surveyors however will go a stage further here and carry out a little test which can move opinion to fact (remember that?). This test (Fig 15) is destructive and involves removing a tiny sliver of gelcoat across the crack thus exposing the underlying laminate. This would never be carried out above the waterline but some surveyors may do it below, or you may be lucky enough to find an area where a chip is already loose.

FUNDAMENTAL REPORT WRITING PRINCIPLE NUMBER TWO
When a conclusion is drawn in a report as the result of a limited sampling, that sampling MUST be fully defined in the report and it must be made quite clear that the conclusion is based on a limited sampling.

Fig 15: Further examination of gelcoat crazing for laminate fracture. A tiny sliver of gelcoat has been removed across the crazing and when examined under X10 magnification it can be seen that there is some cracking extending into the laminate. This is a serious defect and the recommendation would be to grind back to sound laminate before re-laminating.

Fig 16: It is important what type of magnification is used and I have found the Ruper X10 type, obtainable from opticians, to be excellent.

It is necessary to pause here and consider exactly what we have done in order to establish another principle. We come to a conclusion about an area of gelcoat crazing or cracking based on a limited sampling and this is a recurring theme throughout the survey process. The most obvious examples are when assessing moisture content of a hull based on a small number of areas sampled, or ultra sound thickness testing on a steel hull.

Solid FRP layup with structural frames and stringers etc integral with inner mouldings bonded to the shell moulding

Fig 17: Cracked floor pan moulding.

This is now the most common form of construction amongst volume producers because the inner mouldings offer a clean shiny interior to the hull and provide some of the furniture and a basis to which other pre-fabricated furniture units are attached. Bulkheads are often located in moulded channels in the inner moulding and glued in place. This form of construction is the most difficult to survey because the inner moulding is simply lowered into the hull moulding and fixed to it using various types of adhesive between the hull and inner moulding. Therefore much of the structural strength is dependent on the inner mouldings (which contain the frames, stringers etc) staying firmly bonded to the shell moulding but very little of the actual bond will be accessible. The state of this bond is also virtually impossible to test. Hammer sounding inside the boat in key areas such as the keel root may reveal hollow sounding areas where the two mouldings should obviously be firmly joined together but this is usually an inclusive and incomplete test. Video inspection scopes and digital cameras with a long flexible probe are invaluable in this application if some way into the cavity between the two mouldings is available in the form of limber holes or openings for pipework and cable ducting. Given the difficulty of surveying this vital bond I think the time will come where small holes are routinely drilled into the inner moulding to gain access. I have done this, with the Owners permission of course, where serious de-bonding is suspected.

Sometimes the floor pan inner moulding is not continuous, ie it has horizontal flanges in contact with the hull moulding which are then laminated into the hull. This type of bonding is thus visible and any failure should be obvious.

Such floor pan mouldings are also subject to fractures as illustrated in Fig 17. What may appear as inconsequential crazing may actually be a fracture right through the moulding.

This floor pan moulding had some cracking which could easily be overlooked but when tested with a spike the laminate was found to be completely fractured. This was located close to the base of the mast compression post and keel root and is a significant structural defect. This type of damage is commonly seen in modern yachts with deep fin keels which are unable to stand accidental grounding on a hard sandbank in a moderate swell without sustaining some damage.

Part sandwich construction

Quite a few production hulls are now of sandwich construction utilising a foam or end grain balsa core, either over most of the hull or just in the topsides. Such methods produce a lighter stronger panel for a given amount of resin and as such are likely to increase as resin costs escalate. Sandwich construction can usually be identified from inside the boat by a step at the point where the thicker sandwich laminate reverts to solid FRP. This is commonly seen around the waterline, approaching the centreline, or around skin fittings which are often clustered together. The two most serious defects one is likely to encounter are delamination and moisture ingress to the core material. Hammer sounding of the hull must be most thorough, as must the use of appropriate moisture meters to identify any ingress to the core material. Any damage to the hull which has been subsequently repaired becomes more important because large amounts of moisture may have entered the core material and then been sealed in by the repairs.

We will return to the testing of this type of laminate later in this chapter and will also look at some case histories.

In practice one will encounter many hulls that utilise a combination of the above methods and it is of paramount importance from the outset to look at each part of the vessel and understand how it is put together. Only then can the various components one is examining be put into the context of the overall structure. So think beyond the visible parts and take a while to absorb the type of build and how it all works together as a structure. Once this mindset is established it becomes more obvious where structural defects are most likely to be found.

3. DECK AND SUPERSTRUCTURE BUILDING METHODS MOST COMMONLY FOUND IN FRP PRODUCTION SMALL CRAFT

Solid FRP layup with moulded beam reinforcing

This is the simplest form of construction but is heavy and material intensive. Solid FRP is not an ideal material for producing large flat unsupported panels as commonly found in decks and superstructures, so various reinforcing is incorporated into the moulding usually in the form of semicircular beams and longitudinals. Like the thick solid hulls described above the material is at its most reliable in this simple form. However, flexing either side of the various supporting beams and bulkheads just as illustrated in Fig 14 is common. Gelcoat crazing and laminate fracturing around load bearing fittings is also common.

FRP sandwich construction utilising a foam or end grain balsa core between two layers of solid FRP

This is by far the most common form of construction and the majority of small craft built in the last 20 years will have this type of deck etc which produces a much stiffer panel using less resin and being much lighter. No wonder it's attractive to production builders. Many surveyors still do not (or are unable to) distinguish between this form of construction and simple solid FRP layup, and in not doing so they are giving their clients a very poor service and laying themselves open to litigation. So how do we establish what kind of deck we are dealing with? If it is of sandwich construction it will usually revert to solid near the hull deck join where a step can be seen, as shown in Fig 18.

Always also look for any hole through the deck where the raw edge might be visible. This can commonly be seen after removing plastic trims around ventilators etc. Note how the balsa core to the left in Fig 22 is basically dry and clean, while running from the middle to the right it is sodden and rotten. Another commonly seen sign indicating a cored deck is a slight indentation around deck fittings where the tension of fixing bolts has crushed the core material. Where load bearing fittings are through bolted the core should be substituted with plywood or aluminium but often isn't. In this context look for fittings that are not original; these will often be fastened through the core which may be getting crushed and leaks via the fixing bolts will also be likely.

Fig 18: Change from sandwich to solid construction. This is typical of how the step looks as the laminate changes from sandwich to solid. This is also how the change appears in a cored hull as described in the last section.

Fig 19: In unlined areas you can often see the balsa or foam core material.

Fig 20: Section through a horizontal sandwich moulding where it becomes a solid laminate as it runs into the vertical panel. Notice the fillet within the laminate so the change is gradual without creating a hard spot – this is how it should be done but the change is very difficult to spot.

Fig 21: Balsa core sandwich laminate as it should look but often doesn't.

Fig 22: Section of laminate exposed by removing a trim.

So we can see in Fig 22 what can happen to the balsa core when it becomes sodden and in this context also think about cored hulls. Get a nice clear image of rotting cores permanently fixed in your brain now, because anywhere moisture can enter the core there is potential for serious deterioration like this, which is a sobering thought. We will return to this topic in terms of how to trace moisture in cored structures when we look at the use of moisture meters but for now consider for a moment or two just how important it is to establish exactly what kind of construction we are dealing with from the outset, and the consequences of getting it wrong.

FRP sandwich construction overlaid with teak

This is a common variation on the standard cored deck and must be carefully inspected. The vast majority of modern yachts with teak overlay simply have the teak bonded in place and this gives very little trouble. You still have to examine the teak very carefully for excessive wear, which will lead to insufficient depth remaining in the seams to retain the paying.

However, thousands of production yachts have been built in the past where the teak strakes or planks are screwed to the structural deck and every screw driven through the top solid FRP laminate provides a potential path for moisture to enter the foam or, more commonly, balsa core. A screwed deck can be easily identified by the plugs covering the fastenings. And all this takes place unseen under the teak with no obvious signs, just waiting to ruin any unsuspecting surveyor's career. So if you come across a worn teak deck, and in particular to the extent that there is insufficient thickness left to retain the plugs covering the screws, then beware. You can usually see the original thickness close to a deck fitting like a stanchion base or pulpit foot where countless scrubbings over the years plus normal traffic have not

Fig 23: Damaged sandwich construction deck in way of pushpit base. In this case the sharp edge of the base plate to the right of the base has actually cut through the top solid FRP and water can freely enter the core here. Moisture readings around this foot were off scale for a radius of about 12".

worn the deck. Look at Fig 25 which shows missing plugs and failed paying in the seams and imagine what may be going on in the core of this deck.

Note that some production boats utilise a variation on this whereby screws are used to hold the teak in place while the glue sets, and then they are removed with the holes being filled with epoxy then plugged over. However, when this type of deck wears it is obvious that no screws are in place if the plugs come adrift.

Where the plugs have leaked long term the stainless steel screws holding the teak in place will also corrode heavily where they pass through the damp teak causing the material to lift. This is happening in Fig 25.

Let's zoom in on this deck. It's got it all, heavy wear, missing plugs, splits around the fastenings and the paying in poor condition. It will leak like a sieve, straight into the balsa core.

In fact the picture in Fig 22 was taken inside this boat and the condition of the balsa core was poor over the entire deck.

At this stage the deck is structurally unsound and incredibly costly to repair. A far more common scenario is that some ingress around the fittings is detectable by moisture meter but there are no signs of delamination or structural failure under hammer sounding. In fact this is almost inevitable around load bearing fittings in older boats, and both the plywood filling piece and adjacent balsa core will have absorbed moisture. It is however disproportionate to recommend complete rebuilding of the deck when it is still sound but damp inside. A sensible recommendation is to re-bed the fittings to prevent further ingress and to monitor for any change.

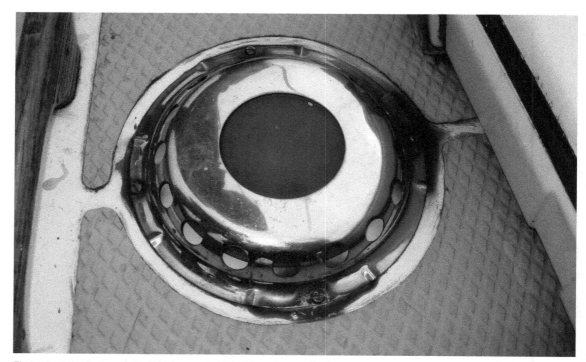

Fig 24: Leaking deck vent. The self tappers holding this vent cover in place are just driven into the deck and through to the core. Never just think in terms of deck leaks, but is it leaking into the core as well?

Of course it's easy when there is a convenient ventilator or similar nearby but that is rarely the case. With cored structures it is necessary to take moisture readings over the exterior surface and we must use a moisture meter capable of detecting deep-seated moisture, not just that in the relatively dry FRP top lamination of the sandwich. However, this is not possible with a teak overlay as the readings will of course be false due to moisture in the teak. So under those circumstances we look for areas inside the boat where the deckhead is not lined, typically large cockpit lockers and chain lockers, to take readings on the underside of the deckhead, but beware of condensation and general damp in such areas giving false readings. In many cases practically all the deckheads will be lined and our only option if the teak is worn and we suspect leaks is to recommend removal of linings for further investigation. This will win you few friends amongst brokers and owners but sooner or later will probably save your career while greatly enhancing your reputation with your clients.

If you have obtained a few satisfactory moisture readings inside the boat on unlined parts of the deck you are going to be thinking about something very important when writing the report, aren't you? Here it is again:

You can clearly see why this principle is so important!

FUNDAMENTAL REPORT WRITING PRINCIPLE NUMBER TWO
When a conclusion is drawn in a report as the result of a limited sampling, that sampling MUST be fully defined in the report and it must be made quite clear that the conclusion is based on a limited sampling.

Fig 25: Teak deck laid over FRP.

Fig 26: Very tired teak deck.

There is one other variation on these teak decks and that is where the 'teak' is not teak at all but merely teak-faced plywood in pre-cut panels with fake seams included. This material wears very quickly and the plywood deteriorates. It is a massively expensive job to replace, requiring the removal of all deck fittings.

It can usually be recognised by a line of staggered butts or joints in each individual 'plank' running across the deck at approximately 8ft intervals. Many later Westerly yachts have this type of deck.

I have deliberately laboured this point as it is potentially one of the most serious defects you will encounter in FRP production boats, and one still missed by many surveyors.

4. BALLAST KEELS AND ASSOCIATED REINFORCING

In the early days of FRP boatbuilding the majority of production yachts had full length or at least long fin keels which faired gently into the hull or, in the case of bolted on keels, had a long and broad root spreading the loadings over a large area. This type of simple design and engineering by and large gave little trouble. Sections aft of fin keels also tended to be veed in section, which is an inherently strong shape when compared with a flat panel.

Look at most modern yachts and you will immediately see how radically things have changed. Deep short keels with minimal attachment area, coupled with almost completely flat sections aft of the keel, are the norm. In simple engineering terms this is probably the worst combination and consequently an area where serious defects are commonly found.

At this stage it is worth thinking about the stresses concentrated in this region. Obviously the hull must be very strong where the keel is attached, but less obvious are the stresses affecting that area immediately aft of the keel. If the boat runs aground at speed and the leading edge of the keel (at its base) makes contact with a solid object, the impact will exert a downward force on the hull immediately forward of the keel and an upward one in that part of the hull immediately aft of the keel as the whole keel tries to hinge aft and upward. As described above, modern yachts typically have very flat sections here which is not an inherently strong shape in FRP.

There are two common types of keel construction used in production building:

Encapsulated keels

Here the shape of the keel is incorporated into the FRP moulding and the space simply filled with ballast. Ferrous metals are the most commonly used and will vary from iron castings made to approximately fit the space to steel punchings or other scrap. The material is usually encapsulated in resin although cement will also be encountered.

Lead is sometimes used but being much more expensive is less common. It is by far the better choice for all keels, being heavier for the same volume (iron 450 lbs per cubic ft, lead 700), and not subject to corrosion.

If you are unsure what material is in the keel, run a magnet along the surface externally: if it is ferrous it will be magnetic. Where the laminate is very thick this may not be detected so double check by holding a small compass close to the keel, this will be deflected if the ballast is ferrous.

The most common defect encountered is where for some reason or another water has entered the space occupied by the ballast. This will not usually be obvious because inside the boat this space is heavily

Fig 27: Laminate splitting due to water ingress to ferrous ballast.

FRP overlaminated and any ingress to the keel space and ballast will not enter the main bilges. The problems arise when the ballast is ferrous (which due to price is the most common), which then rusts over a long period. Fig 27 shows a bilge keeler with encapsulated ballast where the build up of rust has reached a point where it is causing the laminate to actually split. So any signs of rusty water weeping from the keel area, or past stains suggesting this, must be treated very seriously. This is not going to be easy to spot if fresh primer or antifouling has been applied or any splits have been filled and covered up. So again look for any evidence of filler and repair.

In this case it is clear that the laminate is splitting and some weeping has occurred. Filler has also been applied elsewhere, but with new antifouling in place this would not be so obvious. Hammer sounding these areas would reveal where the laminate has split but due to the fact that voids are often present from new around encapsulated ballast the test is not conclusive.

The most common cause of this type of defect is where abrasion damage has occurred in the past, which is obviously quite common on the bases of the keels. This may have subsequently been repaired, but with enough moisture trapped inside the keel for rust to develop. So wherever possible carefully examine the underside of the keel – in this case it was necessary to use a mirror. If you cannot access the underside of the keel, ie where the boat is standing on her keel or keel blocks, be sure to record that fact in your report

Because of the difficulty in drying out this kind of damage you will often encounter bodged repairs to the lower part of encapsulated keels, so be sure to lightly hammer sound such repairs for any voids and de-bonding. Also carefully check the perimeter of the repair where any new laminations finish; see if you can force a blade under the new material due to poor adhesion.

Fig 28: Ballast encapsulation inside a boat breaking up.

Where a bilge keeler is kept on a drying mooring, particularly where the bottom is hard, this kind of damage is common. Under such circumstances a good recommendation to make is the fitting of sacrificial shoes to the undersides of the keels. These can be simple hardwood pads cut to the profile of the keels and epoxy bonded in place. The top surface of the timber is simply covered with thickened epoxy and the boat lowered onto the shoes.

The underside of the moulded keel can be very variable in thickness and liable to damage where it is too thin. Obviously as much of this region should be examined as possible. So let's go aboard this boat (Fig 28).

Not a pretty sight is it? Hammer sounding of the encapsulation covering the ballast revealed an obvious void and gentle prising with a chisel produced this. All that was keeping this boat afloat was a thin layer of de-bonded and degraded FRP, which was about to fail. The rusting is clearly extensive and presents a major problem in terms of repair. However, boats with this defect are frequently bodged up and appear back on the market quickly. So if you find any repairs in this region, however good they appear, advise your client to make further enquiries with the broker or owner as to any supporting documentation. In fact that is sound advice to bear in mind with any alleged repair, maintenance, replacements etc. A genuine conscientious owner will keep all invoices etc, a bodger will not.

Bolted on keels

On production boats these will nearly always be of cast iron or lead, (please not steel as sometimes seen in survey reports). The keel itself will generally give little trouble but lead is obviously quite soft and vulnerable to damage running aground or hitting a hard object. Occasionally one sees a lead keel that is very badly distorted as a result of accidental damage and little can be done about this. Less serious local damage to lead can be repaired by 'dressing in' new material with a blowtorch and the results can be very good.

So it's an obvious point but with all bolted on keels always check that the keel is vertical and square in relation to the hull. Look thoroughly for any damage and consider how any damage may have transferred stresses to other parts of the structure and then carefully examine those areas.

If as is often the case the boat is being lifted out of the water specifically for the survey and you have the opportunity to be present, be there if possible. You may notice that when the boat is hanging in slings an appreciable gap opens up between the hull and keel while the bolts are in tension but this is obviously closed up when the boat is later standing on her keel(s).

Whatever the circumstances are while you examine this vital joint, be sure to specify them in your report together with any restrictions, in accordance with fundamental report writing principle number 3.

FUNDAMENTAL REPORT WRITING PRINCIPLE NUMBER THREE
Areas that could not be accessed for any reason must be defined. PI insurers will normally insist that a general limitation is included in your reports but you should go further than this in important areas and state it again.

It is sometimes necessary to re-bed keels due to seepage up the bolts but the bolts or studs themselves rarely need replacing. If there is minor seepage it is often sufficient to remove the nuts and backing plates then re-bed them on a good quality mastic such as Sikaflex 291. The nuts should be lightly tightened on completion of the job and really hard again 24 hours later. While this may not be considered best practice in comparison with removal and re-bedding of the keel, it offers a much less expensive option and is perfectly acceptable provided the combined tensile strength of the bolts compared with keel weight offers a generous safety margin. I have never known a keel to come off an FRP boat simply as a result of the bolts corroding away.

Where nuts are badly corroded and a large socket spanner will no longer fit sufficiently well to remove the nuts, they can be removed as follows:

Dot punch for a series of holes about 3/16" in diameter radiating out across the wall of the nut, then drill the holes as closely as possible.

The nut can then be split using a heavy club hammer and sharp cold chisel; this also releases the old nut cleanly from the stud without damaging the threads.

The reinforcing over the keel root will be similar whether the keel is encapsulated or bolted on and is basically as described in chapter 2.

We will leave this subject at this stage; the practical section covering keels contains more information concerning testing etc but for the moment just think about the stresses and strains concentrated in this vital area.

CHAPTER 4: **MOISTURE RELATED DEFECTS: RECOGNITION AND DETECTION**

Much of this section is my own opinion developed over many years but it may differ from that of other surveyors. The information below is not necessarily the best or only way but it is the product of many years of practical experience and an overriding wish to offer clients clear and accurate information, not hypothetical jargon or scaremongering.

Every FRP hull will absorb moisture if it is afloat. That is an unavoidable fact and the only way to prevent moisture ingress is to keep the vessel ashore, not a popular option where boats are concerned. By and large, if the laminate is soundly moulded it will take many years before this absorption is of any consequence. However, that is not the public perception and many potential boat owners consider that the most important task of the surveyor is to confirm whether or not the vessel has 'osmosis', or to assess when she is likely to develop it.

Enormous double standards operate where 'osmosis' or 'high moisture content' are suggested, and many buyers will use any such information to beat the price down. After the hapless vendor has agreed to this and the boat changes hands the new owner will often ignore the information and happily use the vessel for years.

⬤ BASIC DEFINITIONS

Osmosis: Tendency of a solvent, when separated from a solution by a suitable membrane (often animal or vegetable), to pass through the membrane so as to dilute the solution. (Oxford Illustrated Dictionary)

The definitions below are all in the context of surveying FRP small craft and are my own.

High moisture content: When sufficient moisture has been absorbed by the underbody for the risk of moisture related defects developing to have become significant.

Moisture related defects: Actual physically detectable changes brought on by the absorption of moisture, such as wicking, blistering and delamination.

Physically detectable: Signs that can be detected during the course of a routine Pre-Purchase Survey without destructive testing or chemical analysis, i.e. what we do on a daily basis.

Note that by these definitions high moisture content in isolation is not a defect.

A chemist will of course tell you that the presence of any moisture will trigger some change in a polyester laminate but we are not chemists nor can we destroy a laminate in order to establish the extent of any changes in the course of a routine survey.

A surveyor's job is to find defects during the course of this routine non-destructive survey. He may also warn of potential defects because of high moisture content, but when it is in isolation with no accompanying physical signs such warning should be measured and realistic, not blatant scaremongering and back watching as is so often the case.

So let's have a look at the most common physical moisture related changes (defects) found in solid FRP hulls. Remember these are actual physical changes which can be detected during the course of a normal survey. Once we can detect and accurately recognise these changes we are well on the way to carrying out a surveyor's primary role, finding defects, and when we have a basic understanding of what has caused them we can begin to quantify the defects in terms of seriousness to the client.

AERATION OF THE GELCOAT

We'll start with a common defect that relates right back to the first section in the previous chapter and the creation of the material. This defect was caused during the very first stage of the moulding process when the 'boat' was still in the resin barrels and on the rolls of glass reinforcing. It is not strictly speaking a moisture related defect although the absorption of moisture often causes it to become visible and thus a physically detectable defect.

Aeration of the gelcoat (also known as double gelcoat blistering) is caused by tiny air bubbles being trapped in the gelcoat mix (or between multiple coats) when it is painted onto the mould surface prior to moulding the boat. In days gone by (and still in some moulding shops today) the gelcoat resin and catalyst are mixed up by hand in a bucket and the mixing process introduces thousands of tiny air bubbles into the liquid which is thixotropic, or 'treacle like' in simple terms. The gelcoat mix should then be left long enough for the air bubbles to rise to the surface of the thick liquid and disperse, but this is often overlooked. We can see the results in Fig 29 as tiny voids, now slightly swollen by the ingress of

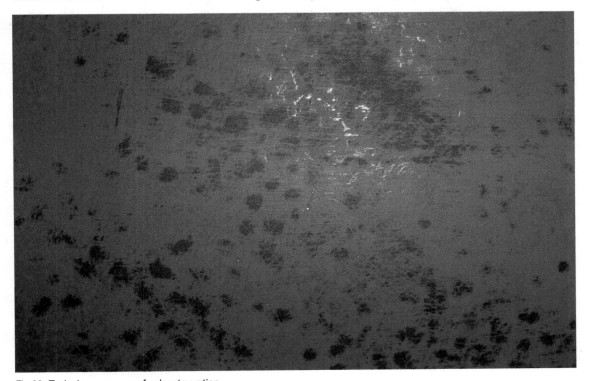

Fig 29: Typical appearance of gelcoat aeration.

moisture, and this has the appearance of a densely packed rash with the circular voids typically 2–4mm in diameter.

It is important to understand that these voids are within the gelcoat itself as opposed to being between the gelcoat and laminate as, for example, with a true osmotic blister.

This condition is often wrongly described as 'osmosis' or 'osmotic blistering' but as we can see it was created long before the boat ever saw water, in fact it occurred before the boat even existed.

How serious is it? Well, where a number of these voids are grouped closely together through the gelcoat they provide a more ready path for moisture to pass right through to the laminate, but equally that moisture can readily dry out if the boat is stored ashore out of season.

Boats usually live with this condition for years without developing serious laminate defects but as ever that is dependent upon the quality of the moulding. So of course it is recorded (and accurately described) in the survey but it is most definitely not osmotic blistering and not treated as such.

With this defect present, the normal advice would be to always store the boat ashore out of season to allow some natural drying out and to monitor the situation annually.

Fig 30: Aeration of the gelcoat with aeration voids broken open.

Just to be clear, Fig 30 shows an area where the various coatings and antifouling have flaked off and aeration can be seen. Some of the voids have broken open and others have not, but where they have broken it can quite clearly be seen that they are voids within the gelcoat itself, not between the gelcoat and laminate as with a conventional osmotic blister.

This condition is also sometimes seen on mouldings above the waterline where hot sun has caused the air in the voids to expand and slightly raise the surface. It is never a structural defect if one defines this as any defect that affects structural integrity, as I do.

● WICKING

Fig 31: Wicking.

Fig 31 is typical of the appearance after removal of the antifouling. This is a straightforward process and is the take up of moisture by capillary action. What appear as single filaments of glass are in fact composed of microscopic strands bundled together. Moisture permeates through the gelcoat and is taken up by these bundles as a result of capillary action, and they eventually swell causing the gelcoat to be raised slightly, and the condition becomes visible to the naked eye. Moulders realised long ago that the incidence of wicking and other moisture related defects can be reduced by applying a thin layer of very fine and light glass cloth (known as surface tissue) directly to the gelcoat as the first layer in the moulding process. This fine layer of glass can be more thoroughly wetted out, i.e. there are less microscopic voids left to take up moisture. So the better quality and more recent laminates are less prone to this defect.

This defect can sometimes appear quite similar to aeration of the gelcoat described above. However, there is one fundamental difference: the shape of the visible raised areas, which are round in the case of aeration of the gelcoat whereas with wicking there will be elongated areas due to the moisture travelling along the glass strands. The difference can clearly be seen in Figs 29 and 30. Eventually the glass strands swell to the point that they begin to break away from the surrounding resin forming small blisters, and where a number of fibres intersect more rounded and large blisters will often be present. This can be seen in Fig 32, which shows a boat with an unpigmented gelcoat below the waterline which conveniently allows us to see into the laminate and examine the wicking in more detail.

The white lines can clearly be seen where moisture is travelling along the fibres, causing them to swell and forming voids around the fibres. Just above and to the left of centre, the larger round white area is where a number of fibres intersect and a larger blister is forming.

At this stage the wicking voids and the embryonic blister will be damp or fluid filled but this will not be under pressure as with a fully formed osmotic blister. However, at this stage all the conditions are in place for the true osmotic process to begin.

This looks worrying, how serious is this wicking?

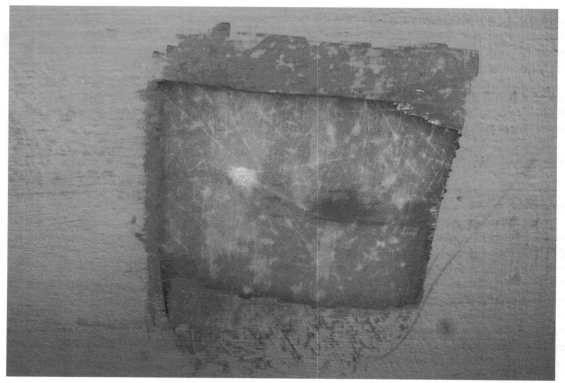

Fig 32: Advanced wicking.

With this defect it's very much a question of degree. In its early stages it is not particularly serious but should be reported and the comment made that as the condition progresses it may become serious and require remedial action. Once fibres are breaking away from the surrounding resin there is obviously a loss of structural strength. If it is accompanied by blisters as in Fig 32, it should be described as serious and requiring remedial action.

In very simple terms it has two stages:

a) Where it has become visible to the naked eye (and thus physically detectable by our definitions at the beginning of this section) and the appearance is like that in Fig 31. At this stage moisture readings will be somewhat higher than areas not affected but often still not at alarming levels. At this stage it does not require any attention but it cannot be reversed. It should be correctly recorded in the report with the advice to always store ashore out of season and to monitor on an annual basis.

b) In stage two it appears more like Fig 32 and because fibres are breaking away to a greater extent it is having some effect on the strength. Osmotic blisters are also forming with the risk of further laminate damage occurring if left untreated.

Fig 32 shows a clear gelcoat we can see into; what can we do if it is a pigmented gel as in Fig 31?

There is a simple test to differentiate between these two stages. Take a spike and test the small raised areas by pressing the spike into the area at an angle of about 45 degrees. If stage two has been reached, where significant voids are forming around the swollen fibres you will hear a slight crunching and cracking sound as you depress the gelcoat surface. The other obvious factor in assessing the seriousness is how widespread over the underbody is the condition, and that applies to all these moisture related defects. These will usually not be visible through the antifouling so small sample patches are removed at random around the underbody for close examination of the underlying surface and the recording of moisture readings. Remember we only remove antifouling and its primer and not epoxy coatings unless previous arrangements have been made with the owner.

As a rule of thumb I remove 2.5 patches for each metre of length overall, and those patches will measure approx 70mm x 70mm. So report any defect such as wicking as a percentage, so on a 10 metre boat remove about 25 patches and you might report as follows:

'The antifouling was removed at random in 25 areas approx 70mm x 70mm for the examination of the underlying surface and recording of moisture readings. In 20% of the areas where antifouling was removed minor wicking was noted. Based on this sampling it is considered that the wicking is localised at this time. In all other areas the exposed gelcoat surface was found free from visible defect.'

Note the phrase free from visible defect: this is quite different from saying the surface was found in good condition. We will return to this later in the report writing chapter. Note also the word sampling, once again we are mindful of Fundamental Report Writing Principle number two (page 30), i.e. we are drawing a conclusion based on a limited sample.

Wicking can sometimes be present close above the waterline, usually in older boats which have been afloat for years. In Fig 33, moisture is spreading up through the laminate from the waterline.

Fig 33: Wicking travelling up from the waterline.

● OSMOTIC BLISTERING

The process of osmosis in FRP craft is well understood and has been much described elsewhere, so this book will concentrate on diagnosis and detection, the surveyor's prime tasks.

Of the defects described so far, osmotic blistering is the easiest to detect once it has reached the point where blisters have formed. These are often easily visible even through thick layers of antifouling. True osmotic blisters will vary in diameter from a few mm up to about 75 mm, although 15–25mm is most typical. If you suspect this kind of blistering, the most important thing to establish straight away is where the blister is located, i.e. if it is within the various coatings on the bottom or if it is a true osmotic blister between the gelcoat (or epoxy coating if the boat has had a previous osmosis treatment) and laminate. Blisters should be opened up at random and the underyling surface examined to determine whether it is the laminate or one of the coatings. If the blisters are obvious, goggles should be worn when carrying this out because the fluid within can be under great pressure, certainly sufficient to propel a jet of noxious fluid into your eye.

True osmotic blisters will contain a fluid denser than water because the moisture has combined with various solutes within the laminate. The fluid will have a pungent vinegary smell and a sticky texture. A ph test will usually find the fluid to be slightly acidic.

Sometimes one comes across blisters that have the appearance of osmotic blisters and the fluid within is similar to that described above. However, when opened up these are found to be in the coatings themselves and are usually due to solvent entrapment from the antifouling. Obviously this type of blistering must not be confused with osmotic blistering and great care must be taken to correctly establish where the blister lies.

At the beginning of this section I said that osmotic blistering is the easiest of these defects to detect, once it has reached the point where blisters have formed.

So how do we detect osmotic blistering when embryonic blisters are present but not yet visible to the naked eye? This is a critical stage and clearly of great interest to any potential purchaser – the last thing he wants is to be paying for a full osmosis treatment six months after purchasing the vessel.

● WHAT MEANS OF DETECTION DO WE HAVE?

Basically there are three: visual examination, scraping away antifouling and moisture readings. Hammer sounding will also reveal very large osmotic blisters (and interlaminar blistering) but by that advanced stage there would be obvious physical signs.

Let's look at these three means of detection in more detail.

Visual examination

Firstly, this type of blistering does not develop at a uniform rate over the entire underbody. So if you have high moisture content (and we will come back to that later in this chapter), particularly in an older boat it is likely that thorough inspection will locate some blistering if the osmotic process is underway. In this respect the visual examination of the underbody must be extremely searching. In particular it must not just consist of a single thorough examination at the beginning of the survey or wherever it fits into your pattern of working. What can be detected by eye will vary greatly as the light conditions change, so what might not be visible at the beginning of the entire survey may be easily detected at the end. So make multiple visual examinations throughout the survey. By far the best conditions for detecting blisters are in the evening when the sun is low and the shadows long. Sometimes a powerful spotlight shone along the hull can be used to replicate these conditions.

Scraping away antifouling

This is a vital process in detecting early blistering. Firstly the tools. It is vitally important to use a very sharp scraper with sufficient width of blade, and the type of vacuum scraper with reversible tungsten-tipped blade previously described in the tools section is ideal.

Osmotic blistering and the other moisture related defects described here all have one thing in common in terms of detection, i.e. they all raise the surface of the gelcoat or epoxy coating. In this context, scraping away antifouling is extremely important because provided you use the correct type of scraper with a perfectly straight wide blade, these defects in their early stages, which cannot yet be seen with the naked eye, will often be revealed.

In Fig 34 the gelcoat surface is only slightly raised and this is not visible to the naked eye. However, as we scrape away the coatings the very sharp and highly honed blade removes the material first where the surface is slightly raised. Think of it like a plane smoothing rough wood, the high spots are removed first. In Fig 34, careful scraping has revealed blisters in varying stages: in the larger white areas the surface is

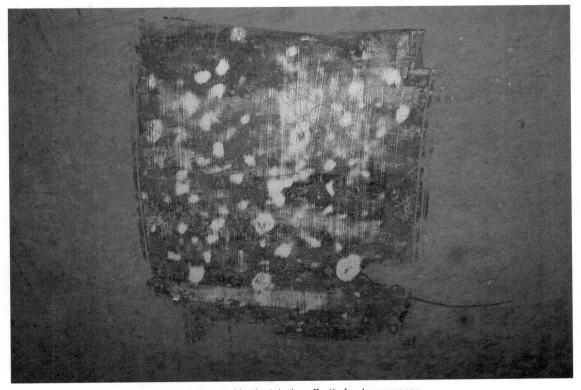

Fig 34: Early stage osmotic blistering only revealed by the 'planing effect' of a sharp scraper.

Fig 35: Sometimes it's easy, you can see the blisters before you get out of your car! The one in the centre of the picture is even weeping, as was the owner.

sufficiently raised so as to be quite clear, whereas others in an earlier stage are only just higher than the surrounding surface but nevertheless their 'peaks' are revealed. Note using any abrasive method such as sandpaper to remove the antifouling or clean up the surface will destroy the effectiveness of this test, as will using a blunt and scored scraper blade.

When osmotic blistering is as advanced and widespread as in Fig 35, we can expect there to be some associated laminate damage and the peeling plus slurry blasting to remove the failed gelcoat may well reveal deep craters and soft laminate. At this point the remedial treatment at least doubles in cost because the defective laminate will have to be removed and the bottom re-laminated with epoxy resin and typically bi- or quad-axial glass cloth. So if you are surveying a boat with advanced osmotic blistering you must always make this quite clear, i.e. removing the coatings back to the laminate may reveal more extensive laminate damage. In fact if you are not confident about this it is sensible to include this warning with every case of osmosis.

We can go a bit further at this stage and carry out a sampling which may give some pointers. I make it routine to open up a number of blisters and sample the state of the laminate within using a spike. Often it is soft and mushy, suggesting laminate damage, and consequent re-lamination is going to be necessary.

This is only a random sampling and the limitations of that sampling must be defined in the report, but I don't need to tell you that now, do I?

Moisture readings

Obviously osmotic blistering cannot have developed without moisture and the use of a moisture meter will show high readings. However, in isolation high readings are not conclusive evidence of osmotic blistering or its imminent development. As we will see in the next section, there are common circumstances where high moisture readings are present without blistering and I have personally seen hundreds of boats over the years that tolerate high moisture content without developing osmotic blistering or any other moisture related physically detectable defect (remember the definitions on page 44).

A few years ago I surveyed one of the earliest production FRP yachts, a Dutch yacht built in 1959, and moisture readings were all off scale. However, the hull rang like a bell under hammer sounding with no physical signs of delamination or voids, and the gelcoat surface was entirely free from visible defect, although not necessarily in good condition. This was a most interesting case because the boat had had so much use over the years that the external gelcoat below the waterline was actually worn away in places, revealing the underlying laminate. Where this was the case it was clear that a very fine glass cloth had been used for the first layer, in exactly the same way as is done today and considered best practice.

In this case the final visible layer inside the boat had been finished with a very fine cloth, probably to make it look better, so in the interests of consistency the first layer immediately behind the gelcoat had also been laminated with this material. So by chance a boat built in 1959 had been moulded using a good practice that did not become commonplace and understood for another 30 odd years.

Fig 36: Degraded hull laminate. Deep craters can be seen bottom right, towards the top left and at the top right of centre. In the event it was necessary to remove 4mm of degraded laminate from the entire underbody.

Fig 37: Blister opened up and showing degraded laminate.

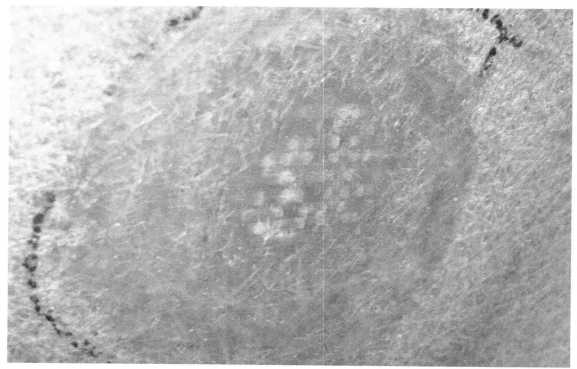

Fig 38: The same area after peeling and grinding. It has been necessary to remove three layers of degraded chopped strand matt back to the woven rovings.

As described earlier in this chapter, where a very fine layer is used immediately behind the gelcoat there is less potential for trapped voids of air and insufficient wetting out, which greatly reduces the risk of later blistering etc and despite very high moisture content over many years in this hull no osmotic blistering or wicking were visible. In my opinion the hull was sound insofar as sufficient structural strength remained, which is another phrase you will become familiar with and which offers a more accurate description under certain circumstances. In this case it could not be argued that changes haven't taken place chemically to this laminate with such a high moisture content but it is still sound and serviceable. We will return to this in more detail in the report writing chapter but undoubtedly you will already be thinking about description and expression and the absolute requirement to be accurate in what is written. Remember again Fundamental Report Writing Principle number one from page 21:

Never confuse fact and opinion.

Fig 39 represents the other end of the scale where wicking and osmotic blistering are present on a hull that has never been launched. The boat had sat in a cradle while the unsuspecting owner completed her from bare mouldings and the cradle supports had been padded with carpet. This had absorbed and retained water over the years, producing eight of these neat patches around the hull.

You will often see a similar effect where wooden rubbing strakes are being replaced on an older boat and moisture has lodged behind them and been retained in the wood.

One of the difficulties encountered when taking moisture readings and examining the underbody for moisture related defects is establishing what (if any) coatings are on the underbody, and whether the boat has had a previous osmosis treatment. When you encounter a vessel with an epoxy coating

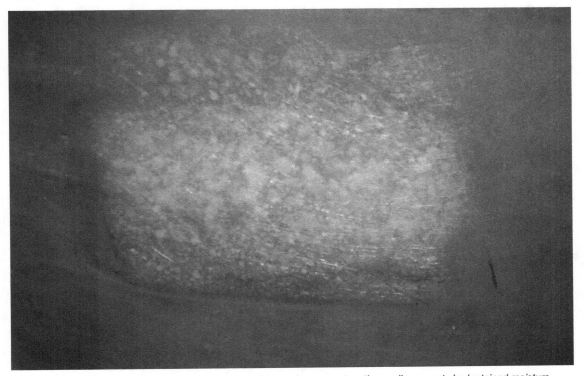

Fig 39: Osmotic blistering and wicking on an unlaunched boat where carpet on the cradle supports had retained moisture.

on the underbody it is obviously preferable to establish whether this is a full osmosis treatment or a preventative treatment applied over the original gelcoat as extra protection against moisture ingress. Where a full osmosis treatment has been carried out, and this is often declared, then enquiries should be made to establish when it was carried out, by whom and whether any current warranty is transferable to a new Owner. Often no history of the alleged treatment is available and under such circumstances the surveyor must be particularly wary.

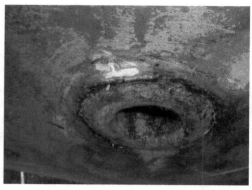

One area where it is often possible to learn more about an osmosis treatment is around skin fittings. These are usually left in place when the treatment is carried out and in particular the original gelcoat is not removed and appears as a ring around the skin fitting. It is obviously vital to confirm that the new coating is at least as thick as the original and this can often be seen at the junction between the original gelcoat and new coatings around a skin fitting.

Fig 40: Reduced hull thickness due to shoddy osmosis treatment.

In Fig 40 this junction can clearly be seen after scraping away a little epoxy (which is on the borderlines of destructive testing). This poor hull is about 4mm thinner than it was before treatment and a step can be seen at the junction of the new and old material. Some attempt has also been made to fair in the difference in thickness and that can be seen through the antifouling in the form of rings radiating out from the fitting where filler has been applied. This hull was so thin as to be structurally unsound but the unwary surveyor could so easily have missed it. However, this was a case where only a quotation for the alleged work (and from a reputable yard) was available, not an invoice. So make sure any documentation you are presented with is what it is claimed to be, as per Fundamental Report Writing Principle number four.

FUNDAMENTAL REPORT WRITING PRINCIPLE NUMBER FOUR
Any documentation concerning improvements or repairs claimed for the vessel must be listed in the report and it MUST be stated whether this documentation was examined or not, and remember, it's invoices, not quotations you need to see

CHAPTER 5: **THE USE AND ABUSE OF MOISTURE METERS**

● USING MOISTURE METERS BELOW THE WATERLINE

Moisture meters are in universal use in the surveying of underwater sections of FRP small craft but in many ways they are unsuitable for this use. Originally these instruments were adapted from the building trade and used to monitor the drying out of FRP hulls prior to osmosis treatment over a long period, and in this application they are a very useful tool. However, in a survey situation their use is limited and much misunderstood. First some basics.

In this application moisture meters cannot:

a) Measure moisture content as a percentage of dry weight as is done with timber, so moisture content is never described as a percentage.

b) Differentiate between plain water and water that has combined with other solutes to form a new denser fluid, i.e. where the process of osmosis is beginning but long before any blistering is evident.

c) Determine whether a 'wet' hull will dry out over a long period.

d) Determine whether a hull will develop osmotic blistering or any other moisture related defect.

Looking at the above we can immediately see how limited these instruments are in the survey of the underbody. Unfortunately there are two more variables that further restrict their usefulness, the period of time the vessel has been ashore, i.e. able to dry out, and the period the vessel was afloat prior to coming ashore. These two facts are vital information and must be taken into account when conducting the survey and of course recorded in the survey report.

And to dispel the common myth: 'She had absorbed so much moisture the poor old crane could hardly lift her.'

The most moisture an average FRP laminate could absorb is about 5% of its dry weight. The wetted area of say an average 10 metre boat amounts to a few hundred kilos of laminate. Forget the overall weight of the boat, it's the few square metres of immersed laminate that are absorbing the moisture. So we are talking about 5% of a few hundred kilos in the worst case scenario. Think about it, if a laminate was of such low density that it could, for example, absorb enough moisture to increase its weight by half, the matrix would be so porous and unsound as to have failed structurally long ago.

The first attempt to relate actual moisture content to percentage increase of dry weight was made by the world famous surveyor Tony Staton Bevan and published as 'Which Moisture Meter' in *Practical Boat Owner* (IPC Magazines) July 1993. Reprints are available from IPC and it is strongly recommended this be obtained.

Here are a few ground rules I have developed over many years and used successfully:

a) In my experience, if the boat has been ashore for less than two weeks in an average British summer or four weeks in winter, moisture readings below the waterline will be affected by harmless surface moisture. Where an epoxy coating is in place these periods should be doubled. If you view the surface of a moulded gelcoat under a microscope it is relatively smooth and void free, the surface having been created when it was painted onto a highly finished and polished mould. Epoxy coatings, however, have been manually applied over that gelcoat by a brush or roller and the surface is full of micro fissures and voids. These take up moisture which is slower to dry out.

b) Most boats built since the early 1990s are a good deal more resistant to moisture absorption due to the use of higher quality isophthalic resins. These will often display low levels of moisture even straight out of the water.

c) Boats stored ashore during the winter are far less likely to have high moisture content for two obvious reasons: they spend less time afloat and have an opportunity to dry out naturally each year. Even in cold weather a strong wind blowing past a hull laid up ashore will draw out moisture.

d) I generally remove about 2.5 patches of antifouling for every metre of overall length, and those patches are about 70mm x 70mm. This is larger than some surveyors but I also want to get a good look at the underlying surface for any wicking, aeration of the gelcoat or blistering. The surface should then be dried if necessary using absorbent kitchen roll. The readings are then taken both above and below the waterline with due regard to condensation and humidity.

The Sovereign Quantum Moisture Meter

This went into production in 2007 and replaced the previous Sovereign Moisture Master. I was involved in the development of this meter and was able to test prototypes alongside other meters over an 18 month period prior to production.

The new meter has a variety of scales but the 0–100 scale is used here with the meter operating in both deep and shallow modes.

The meter has a number of very useful additional functions such as calibration test, measurement of relative humidity, air and substrate surface temperature, and constant monitoring of dew point to warn when unseen condensation may be forming on the substrate being tested. This is all vital information and must be recorded in the survey report.

The meter also has the ability to switch from shallow to deep reading mode while remaining on the same 0–100 scale. On solid laminates, experience shows that if there is no further deep seated moisture the readings will fall slightly because the same level of moisture is being read over a greater depth. So if readings fall or remain the same there is no further moisture. Care must of course be taken when switching to deep mode not to read right through the laminate to bulkheads, damp bilges etc. Full details of this meter and its multiple functions can be found at **www.sovchem.co.uk**.

Original Tramex and Sovereign Moisture Meters

These two instruments were used for many years and the following comments are provided for those who may have some experience of these older meters. They also illustrate their fundamental differences and why it was essential to use both in the past.

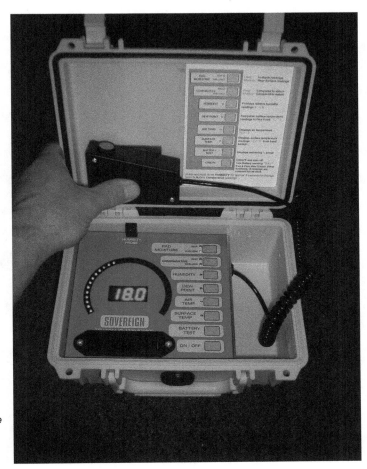

Fig 41: Sovereign Quantum Moisture Meter. Here the self calibration check is being used with the meter operating in shallow mode; the check is also available for deep reading. This check must be performed before each and every use and recorded in the survey report.

Briefly the original Tramex meter would readily detect moisture up to about 10mm deep, while the original Sovereign's response dropped off very rapidly after about 3mm. This broadly corresponds to the Quantum's shallow and deep modes with the major advantage that one identical scale is being used in both shallow and deep modes.

So it is immediately clear that each meter had its uses, i.e. it would be useless using an old Sovereign to detect moisture around leaking deck fittings on say a 10 metre yacht with a heavily laid up sandwich construction deck because the top solid FRP lamination may be quite dry, whereas the core may be sodden (and unsound) where water has leaked down the fixing bolts. Conversely the old Tramex would be of limited use on a small boat with a lightly laid up hull below the waterline and water in the bilges. Neither of these meters had a calibration check and that was also a compelling reason for using two meters.

The Quantum can be quickly checked for calibration before every use.

An understanding of the meters' characteristics is absolutely vital but once fully understood moisture meters become a far more valuable tool. In this respect you are urged to carry out your own experiments and tests.

Fig 42: Quantum detector head. The detector head sits comfortably in the hand and the red button on the side is used to switch between shallow and deep reading modes, providing very quick readings and comparisons to be made.

So now we have our moisture readings, but what do they mean?

Well, the readings usually cover quite a wide range and are always expressed as such. Some surveyors advocate averaging the readings but I have never found it either necessary or helpful.

As described earlier in this chapter, our client considers this one of the most important aspects of the survey. Opinions vary greatly on this issue and I can only describe the methods I have used successfully over a long period.

The figures and associated comments given below would inevitably lead to some discussion amongst any group of surveyors and I must emphasise that you should develop your own opinions. What is stated here are criteria I have developed over many years and which have performed well during that period.

At this point it would be a good idea to think again about our definitions from page 44:

High moisture content: When sufficient moisture has been absorbed by the underbody for the risk of moisture related defects developing to have become significant.

Moisture related defects: Actual physically detectable changes brought on by the absorption of moisture, such as wicking, blistering and delamination.

Physically detectable: Signs that can be detected during the course of a routine Pre-Purchase Survey without destructive testing or chemical analysis, i.e. what we do on a daily basis.

The following interpretations have been defined after using the meter on hundreds of boats. It cannot be stressed enough, however, that you must develop your own opinions on this subject and that can only be done with experience.

The following table applies to the Sovereign Quantum Meter with 3-8 version software installed which became standard from mid 2008. The table relates to solid GRP laminates only.

Interpretation and comment for range of readings when operating on shallow mode 0–100.

0–15	For all practical purposes may be considered dry.
16–20	Some moisture present at low levels but of no great concern.
21–30	Considered medium, but those at the top of that range, i.e. 30 (I always quote the range not average), are at the point where the risk of moisture related defects developing is significant.
31–45	Considered high and at a level where the risk of moisture related defects being present but not yet physically detectable is significant.
46–60	Very high and will usually be accompanied by physically detectable signs. Likely to be accompanied by a significant increase when switching to deep mode.
61–100	Extremely high and indicative of possible laminate damage in addition to osmotic blistering. Likely to be accompanied by a significant increase when switched to deep mode.

These interpretations MUST be considered in conjunction with the period the vessel has been ashore and the weather conditions when the readings were obtained. If the boat has been ashore for less than two weeks in summer and a month in winter (UK), it is reasonable to say in the report that readings can be expected to fall were the vessel to remain ashore for a few weeks (but obviously not when physically detectable signs are also present). The meter constantly monitors degrees above dew point once it has been set up, and when within 3 degrees of this condensation can be expected on the substrate, so constantly dry the surface and the detector pad. As a general rule of thumb experience suggests readings will fall by one range in the above table within a few weeks ashore and two after six months.

Boats built since the early 1990s are generally much more moisture resistant and also dry out quicker. These will often exhibit low readings straight out of the water once the surface is dried off.

The above are guidelines not rules and cannot be applied to every laminate.

If moisture readings are accompanied by even the slightest physically detectable moisture related defect then one must assume that changes are underway in the laminate due to the moisture ingress and report accordingly. The seriousness of those changes should be put into perspective and the descriptions in the previous section will be useful in this respect.

Of course the readings must always be considered in relation to how long the boat has been ashore and what kind of coating is on the bottom. If the boat has only just come out of the water and is showing high moisture content but no physically detectable moisture related defects then one can say that it is considered likely that a significant fall in moisture levels would be achieved were the vessel to remain ashore for some months, for example over a winter lay up period, but that this cannot be guaranteed.

If the vessel is showing high moisture content after having been ashore for a long period then it is most likely that the moisture has combined with other solutes to form a new denser liquid which will not dry out as readily as less dense water. In such circumstances be very wary and advise that the vessel is likely to develop physically detectable moisture related defects within a year of recommissioning.

There are obviously numerous different types and weights of laminate and you should carry out as many tests and experiments as you can to familiarise yourself with your meter's response through various laminates etc. These guidelines should obviously be read in conjunction with the instructions and technical information issued by Sovereign with the meter. These can be found on the website **www. sovchem.co.uk**.

USING MOISTURE METERS TO DETECT MOISTURE IN FRP SANDWICH STRUCTURES

On sandwich laminates below the waterline and in the topsides, any increase in readings when changing from shallow to deep should be treated with great caution and investigated further.

As previously described, the majority of production small craft have a sandwich construction deck utilising either an end grain balsa wood or foam core, in order to produce a stiff flat panel. A few production boats also feature cored hulls.

Having established that the moisture meter has such differing characteristics in terms of depth of penetration in each mode, one can see that it is possible to use the meter on cored structures in order to identify any ingress to the core material. If, for example, one is examining a cored hull and high moisture content is found during the routine use of the meter as part of the external examination, how do we establish whether this is normal ingress to the outer FRP layer as would be found in a solid FRP hull, or ingress to the core, or indeed, both?

The following procedures can be carried out:

a) Use the meter on deep mode and see if there is any difference below the waterline where the laminate changes from cored to solid. If the solid parts display lower readings then one can assume there is some moisture in the core.

b) Take readings on the inside surface of the hull again in solid and cored areas above and below the waterline. Using a methodical approach and exploiting the known and very different depth of penetration between shallow and deep reading modes, it is possible to build up a useful picture of where the moisture is concentrated.

With sandwich construction decks one can expect higher readings on deep mode locally around fittings etc where ingress has occurred, and this must be reported. The correlation between shallow and deep may be different to that found below the waterline, however, because moisture has penetrated via holes rather than through the outer solid FRP laminate due to long term immersion.

This will typically be found around mechanically fastened fittings and in particular those which have been retro fitted some time after the boat was built. This is because most original fittings that carry any load usually have plywood pads built into the laminate (and thus making it solid) where they are to be fitted, but retro fitted items will not have this. So the fixing bolts will often crush the soft core and the item will leak from day one. This is particularly common around turning blocks and organisers on sailing yachts where halyards etc have been led aft to the cockpit.

How serious is such ingress? On an older boat this is a similar situation to high moisture readings in the underbody and if the ingress is localised and not accompanied by any physically detectable defects it warrants a description and warning that further deterioration may occur. As previously described in the section on deck construction, it may be disproportionate to recommend major repairs, particularly as the sandwich core will most likely be plywood in way of the fittings in question if these are original and load bearing.

It is also sensible to mention that, given the form of construction, some ingress over time is inevitable.

OTHER USES FOR MOISTURE METERS IN THE FRP SURVEY PROCESS

Most production boats have some structural plywood components such as bulkheads. If these absorb moisture over a long period then rot may occur. This is particularly important where load bearing fittings are attached, the most common problem area being chain plates or similar. If these have leaked where they pass through the deck (and all load bearing fittings are prone to this), then the plywood bulkhead to which they are attached, and which dissipates the loading into the structure, may be rotting unseen particularly behind the FRP bonding at its perimeter where it is bonded into the hull. Such bulkheads may also be rotting at their bases if bilge water is present.

One situation to beware of is boats that have been sunk and recovered in the past. These may have had thousands spent on them with new linings, upholstery, engines, electrics etc etc but no amount of drying out will remove the moisture behind the FRP where the bulkheads are bonded in and these may quietly rot away unseen. So if you find yourself surveying a boat where so much of the interior and gear is clearly younger than the boat, ask yourself why and use the moisture meter all over the boat's interior. There is no reason why plywood parts well inside the vessel and away from potential sources of moisture should be 'wet'.

The use of moisture meters requires some common sense and practice but given a basic understanding of their characteristics they can be very useful in the survey process. Without that understanding they are useless to the surveyor, who is also likely to mislead the client. You are urged most strongly therefore to continue setting up your own tests and experiments and to take every opportunity to inspect hulls and decks that may be under repair due to moisture related defects, real or imagined!

In the next chapter you will find extracts from past survey reports which illustrate how the information collected using the meter is expressed.

THE SURVEY INSPECTION IN MANAGEABLE STAGES

CHAPTER 6: INSPECTION SECTIONS 1-9

So far we have looked at the basic FRP structure and some of the common defects likely to be encountered. In the remainder of the book we will take each stage of the inspection process in detail, culminating in preparing the report from the information we have gleaned. The following stages of the inspection are presented in the order used for a standard Pre-Purchase Survey Report. Under each heading are points to be checked and particular investigations to be carried out. Where necessary, extracts from past survey reports, illustrating the type of defects that may be encountered and how such information is presented, are also included. If you are more concerned with conducting an inspection for your own use you may wish to skip the report extracts. What follows is essentially a practical stage by stage guide to surveying a typical standard FRP production small craft of about 10 metres, built in the last 20 years. The guidelines are necessarily brief and obviously cannot cover every permutation. It is also intended that this stage by stage approach should serve as an on site aide memoire for those wanting to look at a craft in more depth, whether as a surveyor or potential purchaser.

The list below shows 37 typical sections used in a standard Pre-Purchase Survey Report under seven sub headings. Many of the characteristics and defects likely to be found in sections 1–9 have already been illustrated and discussed in the preceding chapters and reference to the pictures therein will aid recognition of defects. From section 10 onwards numerous illustrations will be provided and discussed stage by stage. In this chapter we will cover sections 1–9.

● HULL, DECK AND SUPERSTRUCTURE
1. Details of subject vessel (general description, dimensions, registration etc)
2. Keel
3. Hull below waterline
4. Topsides above waterline including rubbing strake etc.
5. Deck moulding
6. Coachroof
7. Cockpit
8. Hull/deck join
9. Bulkheads and structural stiffening including internal mouldings

● STEERING, STERN GEAR, SKIN FITTINGS ETC
10. Rudder and steering
11. Stern gear
12. Cathodic protection
13. Skin fittings and other through hull apertures

● ON DECK
14. Main companionway and other accesses to accommodation
15. Ports, windows etc
16. Pulpit, stanchions, pushpit, lifelines and jackstays
17. Rigging attachment points

18. Ground tackle and mooring arrangements
19. Other deck gear and fittings
20. Davits and boarding ladders

● RIG

21. Spars
22. Standing rigging
23. Running rigging
24. Sails and covers etc

● SAFETY

25. Navigation lights
26. Bilge pumping arrangements
27. Firefighting equipment
28. Lifesaving and emergency equipment

● ENGINE AND FUEL SYETEM

29. Engine and installation
30. Fuel system

● ACCOMMODATION AND ON BOARD SYSTEMS

31. Accommodation, general
32. Gas installation
33. Fresh water tanks and delivery
34. Heads
35. Electrical installation
36. Electronic and navigation equipment
37. Heating and refrigeration systems

Before going any further it is worth thinking about the order of work required to complete the inspection thoroughly and efficiently. Methodical working is paramount if the inspection is to be completed to the necessary standard. I start at ground level, then cover everything on deck before working inside the boat. Throughout the inspection it will be necessary to shift from stage to stage and as such the efficient recording of information is vital.

● SECTION 1, DETAILS OF SUBJECT VESSEL

- Record all moulding numbers, HIN numbers and other identifying marks.
- Establish what, if any, mandatory standards apply to the vessel being surveyed.
- Details of any registration plus any potential RCD or VAT issues. Most new pleasure craft put on the market from 15 June 1998 onwards were required to be RCD compliant, look for the CE plate. So if you encounter a boat built post 1998 but not CE marked this will probably require post certification, which is usually a very expensive process. Boats imported from outside the EU economic area since that date are also quite common and most of these boats entering the EU will also require post certification. Such boats may also be liable to VAT. If in doubt, put the client in touch with a specialist or offer to arrange this for him.
- Record general details and dimensions.
- Are any broker's details, inventory etc correct, particularly expensive portable items like liferafts, cruising chutes etc? If details are wrong this must be recorded in the survey report.
- Are there supporting invoices, not estimates or quotations for any major work or replacements claimed?

REPORT EXTRACT

Subject vessel is a standard Prowler class twin screw flybridge motor cruiser built by Cooper Yachts of Canada in 1991. She is a typical design of this general type but was not sold in the UK in any numbers. This example was imported from Canada in 1999 or 2000 by the Vendor and when first put into use in this country would have been subject to the Recreational Craft Directive legislation. However the vessel has not been post certificated to conform to this legislation and as such is being illegally traded by the Vendor. This situation will transfer to any subsequent purchaser and the penalties for breaching the RCD legislation are severe. It is of course also essential to confirm VAT was paid status and whether any import duty applies. It is therefore strongly recommended that specialist advice be sought on the legislation and its implications in this case prior to purchase. (I can advise on suitable specialists if required.)

● SECTION 2, KEEL

First and foremost, is it safe to work under the boat?

- Is too much weight being taken on the keel, thus deflecting the hull around the keel root, or conversely are any of the cradle supports too tight and deflecting the hull?
- If bolted on check joint externally, is keel lying tight and fair to hull? If, as is often the case, the boat is being lifted out of the water specifically for the survey and you have the opportunity to be present be there if possible. You may notice that while the boat is hanging in slings an appreciable gap opens up between the hull and keel while the bolts are in tension but this obviously closes up when the boat is later standing on her keel(s).
- Sight the keel from various angles, is it vertical and square in relation to the hull?
- Any weeps or stains externally?
- Condition of keel surface?
- Material of keelbolts and condition of backing plates/nuts. It is worth noting that most 'keelbolts' are in fact studs either threaded into the keel or cast in and as such removal can be very difficult or in some cases impossible. So recommending of a keelbolt on most modern yachts is not appropriate, the keel usually has to be dropped with the studs remaining in it. (It is best to use the term keelstuds with modern boats.)
- Any sign of seepage inside the boat, look for corrosion plus long term stains in bilges adjacent to bolts. If nuts encapsulated is there any sign of discolouration to the adjacent laminate, typically brown staining where seepage is occurring? Is the diameter of the keelbolts correct for the holes? You will sometimes find the washers distorted into a cup shape where the bolts are of a smaller diameter than the holes and the bolts have been tightened in a vain attempt to stop leaks.

Why has an electric float switch operated pump been fitted in the keel stub?

- Nuts are often FRP encapsulated, look for any staining in the surrounding laminate and bilges, this may indicate seepage. Beware newly painted bilges, is this a sign of a meticulous owner, i.e. are all other lockers and bilges equally clean and well painted, or an attempt to cover up leaking keelbolts.
- If keel is of FRP encapsulated type, is there any damage to keels externally? Hammer sound any external repairs and check carefully the perimeter of such repairs for de-bonding, see if you can force a blade under the edges of the repair.

- If possible look under the keel (use an extending mirror) for abrasion damage, weeps etc. If underside not accessible record this in the report. (This is mainly for damage to encapsulated keels and consequent water ingress.)
- Any sign of ingress to the ballast internally? If so are there any splits or swelling in laminate externally due to build up of rust (where ballast is ferrous)?
- Is keel root reinforcing intact? This takes many forms, i.e. plywood webs bonded in, top hat section floors, frames and floors moulded integrally with the inner moulding etc. Hammer sound the various moulded frames and floors, be particularly on the look out for thin FRP 'repairs' covering serious underlying fractures in the original structural members. Has the area been painted recently, if so why?
- In addition, for lifting keels check any pivot bolts, lifting tackle, winches and condition of lifting pendant where accessible. If any of these items are not accessible be sure to specify this. If the general condition of accessible parts is poor then think about those areas not accessible and recommend further dismantling for full inspection.
- Some boats, particularly motor vessels, may be fitted with a protective shoe bolted through the hull, is this secure and fixing bolts intact?

We looked at rusting ballast in encapsulated keels and associated consequences in chapter 3 section 4 and the following pictures also emphasise again the importance of:

FUNDAMENTAL REPORT WRITING PRINCIPLE NUMBER FOUR
Areas which could not be accessed for any reason must be defined. PI Insurers will normally insist that a general limitation is included in your reports but you should go further than this in important areas and state it again.

Fig 43: Some innocuous looking staining at the base of a moulded bilge keel.

This is the port bilge keel on a large seagoing motor sailer which was about to set off on an extended cruise. The staining at the base of the keel could easily be overlooked and were the boat standing on her bilge keels very little would be visible at all. It is vital to define exactly what could be done in this instance because as we can see in Fig 44, all is far from well.

Fig 44: Use of mirror to examine underside of moulded keel.

As soon as a mirror is placed under the keel immediately aft of the keel support block it is obvious that the laminate is split and the crack runs forward under the keel support block, where the split may be even more severe. Closer inspection of the support block shows it to be brown and stained by rust discoloured water which had been running out of the split for some time in the past. No longer is this a fairly innocuous and unobtrusive stain at the base of a keel, it is a potentially very serious defect and as described in chapter 3 section 4 it will be very expensive to repair. In just 10 seconds using a mirror the entire situation is changed. Oh yes, and it might just sink the vessel if the internal encapsulation has reached the point as seen in Fig 28. Quite a sobering thought because if this boat had been standing on her keels without any blocks the crack would not have been accessible at all. So here it is again:

FUNDAMENTAL REPORT WRITING PRINCIPLE NUMBER FOUR
Areas that could not be accessed for any reason must be defined. PI insurers will normally insist that a general limitation is included in your reports but you should go further than this in important areas and state it again.

REPORT EXTRACTS

Damaged encapsulated keels and consequent leaks

Recent history and observations: Vessel had been launched about a week before this inspection and immediately brought ashore after leaks were discovered across the port bilge keel root. I had previously surveyed this yacht for a prospective purchaser who did not proceed. As far as I am aware the yacht remained laid up and did not move again till she was recently launched having been sold. The following is an extract from the original survey report: The ballast is fully encapsulated within the moulded bilge keels. Underside of keels examined as far as possible and found in satisfactory condition with the exception of the port keel forward end and extending aft about 450 mm. Here a repair has been carried out, probably to some abrasion damage. The repair consists of FRP laminations under the keel, and with some filler at the outboard edge. When hammer sounded the repair found loose, and with water lying beneath.

Recommendation: The defective repair to the port keel should be removed and the keel ground back to sound laminate before re-laminating using epoxy resin. If the vessel is to take the ground every tide it would be worthwhile fitting keel shoes to protect the GRP. These can simply be made of oak or similar hardwood about 50mm thick cut out to the shape of the keel and bonded to the underside using thickened epoxy resin paste.

The above defect is almost certainly the source of the leak and the condition of the defective repair remains unchanged since the last inspection apart from having had a coat of paint applied. At this second inspection the yacht was seen sitting on a cradle with better access to the base of both keels and further repairs could be seen, these mostly on the port keel. Although the other repairs appear to be quite minor and intact given the poor quality of that identified above, it would be prudent to remove all past repairs and carry out refurbishment to both keels. This type of abrasion damage and associated repair is not uncommon with a bilge keel yacht of this age and repairs have been carried out on a piecemeal basis over a long period, but that described above is clearly inadequate. From aboard the boat access was restricted to the roots of the keels but where seen the FRP laminations across the keels are intact and are not seriously degrading due to long term saturation.

Recommendations:
a) The inboard and outboard faces of both keels should be ground out for about 100mm upwards from base to remove all previous filler etc and provide a taper for re-laminating. Sound laminate can be left in place but it is important at this stage to remove any that may be damp to ensure a good bond for the new laminations. The underside of keels should also be keyed and ground out where necessary to receive some additional laminations.

b) It must be accepted that some moisture will remain within the keels given the long term seepage but every effort should be made using local heat to achieve a dry surface prior to re-lamination. It is suggested epoxy resin be used for superior bond and the new laminations to be of a thickness at least equal to the original.

c) Having restored the keels to a watertight and satisfactory condition it is strongly suggested keel shoes be fitted to prevent further damage. Numerous methods are equally successful but a very simple remedy is to bond hardwood shoes cut to shape directly to the underside of the keels using thickened epoxy resin. These should be about 50mm thick and can be of any available hardwood, green oak being suitable and inexpensive. It is also recommended in this case that a similar shoe be fitted to the underside of the long skeg. When fitting keel shoes the use of any mechanical fastenings into the keels should be avoided as these are potential sources of seepage.

Fin keel and defective reinforcing

The fin keel is of cast iron, bolted to the hull moulding with stainless steel bolts. The surface of the keel has become a little pitted and is rusting in places, but this is not serious, and the action to be taken depends on the degree of smoothness required. The best course of action would be to have the iron surface shot blasted and epoxy painted, such a treatment preventing rusting for some years. In between these two options there are many DIY products which are intended to be applied each season and which will inhibit corrosion and provide a reasonably smooth surface.

However if cost is important it would be quite acceptable to do nothing and merely antifoul the keel, the consequent rusting being very slow indeed.

Keel lying tight and fair to hull with no weeps or stains present which would suggest seepage via the keel bolts. The joint has been faired with hard filler and this was removed at random to expose the joint, all found satisfactory. The joint will require minor filling and fairing annually as part of normal maintenance. Seen from aboard the area in way of keel root is stiffened by longitudinal and transverse webs of FRP formed over plywood. This was the standard arrangement in early models of this design but was modified in later examples. Towards the aft end of the keel the hull was seen deflecting inwards very slightly causing the transverse members aft (upon which the aftermost floor sole board rests) to become slightly convex. There is structural damage to the reinforcing webs at the following points:

- Where the two longitudinals port and starboard of the centreline intersect the first transverse member aft of mast position.
- Where the above two longitudinals intersect the next transverse member.
- Where the longitudinal on the port side intersects the aftermost transverse member.

Recommendation: There is structural damage to the web reinforcing in way of the keel root. This will require grinding out and re-laminating using epoxy resin for superior adhesion and strength. Prior to and during repair it will be necessary to support the hull taking some weight off the keel to allow the hull to return to its original shape. These repairs will only return the structure to its former strength, and it is suggested consideration be given to increasing the cross section of the existing webs to add strength, this being the standard arrangement in later examples of this design.

Bilge keel seepage and defective reinforcing

The keels are of cast iron, bolted to the hull moulding with stainless steel bolts. There is some build up of rust and scale on the iron surface but this of little consequence. Both keels seen lying fair to the hull. There is slight wear to the bases of both keels at their aft ends but this of little consequence. Seen from aboard there was access to all of the stb keel root and most of that to port. There is evidence of seepage from both keels and sealant has been applied in way of the bolts on the port side. There has been some movement at the aft end of the stb keel and the FRP bonding to the transverse partition is failing. There have also been some inadequate repairs to the base of the aftermost transverse web on the stb side. To port the bonding has failed on both faces of the forward most transverse partition across the keel stub.

Recommendation: It is clear that seepage has occurred via both keels and some deterioration to the internal reinforcing, (which is original) has taken place. It is thus appropriate at this stage in the boat's life to re-bed both keels and improve the original reinforcing internally as eventually becomes necessary with all examples of this design. Most boatyards will have carried out this work and can offer an approved specification.

Inadequate keel reinforcing and severe hull deflection

The keel is lead, bolted to the hull moulding with stainless steel bolts. The keel is not lying tight to the hull at both fore and aft ends. Forward there is about 1/2" gap running out to nothing over about 9".

Aft the gap is about 1/4" running out to nothing over about 6". The gaps are filled with mastic and have almost certainly been present from new. The keel itself is free from any serious damage, although it was not possible to examine the underside. It was noted that the hull is deflecting inward about 3/8" just aft of the keel. On going aboard it was noted that the sole boards were not lying flat in the saloon. These were all removed to reveal the moulded floor pan module which is bonded into the hull to dissipate keel stresses and mast compression. The module consists of two longitudinals either side of the centreline with 6 transverse members of similar top hat section. Numbers 5 and 6 are quite heavily distorted and stress cracks are present at the following points:

- Where both 5 and 6 transverse members intersect with the two longitudinals.
- Number 6 transverse member is cracked the full length of its forward face running between the two longitudinals.
- Number 4 transverse member has small cracks at its intersection with both longitudinals.

It will be necessary to grind out the cracks to ascertain their depth and severity. It is also of serious concern that the hull and reinforcing members are flexing as one and in addition to mere repair it would be prudent to build in some extra strength.

Recommendation: The cracked areas in the floor pan moulding in way of the keel root as described in the text should be ground out to ascertain their full extent. At that stage the vessel should be further inspected with a view to strengthening the existing structure. It will be necessary to suspend the boat in slings in order that she may return to her correct shape prior to repairs.

Motor vessel with keel shoe becoming detached with potential serious leak.

There is no keel as such in this design, which features a shallow vee semi displacement hull. The centreline and forefoot viewed externally found in good condition with no abrasion damage noted. A protective timber shoe has been fitted to the underside of the long shallow keel and this has split badly both fore and aft. The shoe is bolted through the hull and where the timber has split the securing bolts may become loose in the hull and leak. Elsewhere it would appear that the bolt heads have previously corroded away and simply been filled over with mastic. It is considered essential to check the security of all the bolts, and the method used to seal those areas where bolt heads have previously corroded away.

Recommendation: The position of all the existing bolts securing the keel shoe and the position of any previous bolts now corroded away should be established and their security confirmed. Some of the bolts are accessible inside the boat and it was noted that they are not FRP encapsulated and as such if they corrode away a serious leak could result. It is clear that access to all the bolts from inside the boat will not be possible due to tanks etc and where no access can be gained it is suggested the bolts be cut off and driven inwards then the holes filled with epoxy and overlaminated externally. Those accessible inside the boat can simply be overlaminated inside. The existing timber shoe is an addition to the standard design and would have been regarded as sacrificial. It is not therefore essential to replace the shoe but if that is required it may simply be bonded back in place (in manageable lengths) using thickened epoxy resin. In fact it would probably be possible to re-use the existing timber.

● SECTION 3, HULL BELOW WATERLINE:

- Establish type of construction, typically chopped strand matt plus rovings for ordinary production boats. More modern designs may include Kevlar. Beware of sandwich construction! You can usually see a step in the hull thickness inside the boat where the laminate changes from sandwich to solid close to the centreline, this often visible under the forward berths, or where a seacock is fitted.
- Any hull deflection due to ill fitting cradle supports etc? Laminate damage may already have occurred as a result and you might be held liable if boat is allegedly damaged by your weight moving about on board.
- Lightly hammer sound entire hull listening for any change in note. Most important to find any voids and dry areas in the laminate, (often present from new) or delamination since. If unsure err on the cautious side.
- Check for any sign of damage or repair.
- Check for stress crazing particularly in way of hardspots created by bulkheads stringers etc. If you find crazing try to deflect the hull with the end of a hammer shaft or similar, and compare the stiffness with the corresponding position on the other side of the hull. With high speed motor boats look for crazing
  in the forward and midship sections which may pound at high speeds.
- If a skeg is fitted check carefully where it joins the hull. If moulded integrally with the hull check for stress crazing and in all cases aggressively test the skeg for any movement. If supporting blocks have been placed under the skeg preventing this ask the yard to move them, or specify in report that it was not possible to test the skeg for any flexing or movement.

- Remove antifouling to expose gelcoat or epoxy surface. Carefully inspect surface for visible defects particularly blisters or wicking. If blisters or wicking found test as described in chapter 4.
- Dry the surface and take moisture readings noting the weather conditions and suitability for obtaining readings.

REPORT EXTRACTS

Moisture ingress to foam cored hull

The construction of this hull is quite unusual in that all the topsides and most of the underbody are of foam sandwich construction. No sign of major impact or repair evident through the antifouling or where this was removed. No stress crazing evident around root of keel. Light hammer sounding (not heavy enough to damage the gelcoat), did not suggest any delamination or voids. Vessel was found with only a light build up of old antifouling and this was removed at random in 30 areas approx. 70mm x 70mm, to reveal an epoxy coating. As far as could be ascertained without destructive testing this coating has been applied over the original gelcoat as a preventative measure, in the areas where the coating was exposed it was found free from visible defect and adhering well.

Moisture readings were taken in the areas where the antifouling was removed using a capacitance type moisture meter of Sovereign Quantum type, operating in both shallow and deep reading modes. The meter was first checked for correct calibration. The readings recorded below are from the meter operating in the shallow mode on the relative scale 0–100. Readings were taken both above and below waterline in order to obtain a comparison. The readings are relative and do not express moisture content as a percentage of dry weight. High moisture content is not generally a structural defect, and is to be expected in older boats. However where some moisture has been absorbed the likelihood of moisture related problems occurring is higher, and the actual state of the laminate cannot be completely guaranteed without destructive testing followed by chemical analysis. The opinion given in this survey is based on all the evidence available at the time but without destructive testing. The conditions prevailing when the readings were taken were as follows:

AIR TEMPERATURE:	10.5°C
SURFACE TEMPERATURE:	9.5°C
RELATIVE HUMIDITY:	56%

In summary weather conditions for obtaining moisture readings were good and the vessel had been ashore 4 weeks.

Readings in 25 of the 30 areas where antifouling was removed were as follows:

METER	RANGE BELOW WATERLINE	RANGE ABOVE WATERLINE
Sovereign Quantum 0-100	13–15	15–16

The values recorded above are very low and indicate the presence of very little moisture ingress indeed and where these low levels were recorded the laminate can be described as being in good condition at this time. In the remaining five areas very much higher readings were found, these all on the stb side. In view of this the following procedure was adopted:

The hull was again hammer sounded and the position where the laminate changes from sandwich construction to solid FRP was marked on the hull, this evident by a change in tone of the sounding.

(This point was also confirmed in a few places internally where there was access to the hull and the step in the laminate is visible.) On the stb side very high moisture levels were found in a band coming aft from the leading edge of the keel for about 7' 6". The top of this band was located about 40" up from the keel and extending down about 20". In this area the moisture readings were all off scale.

Within the above area five broad vertical bands of antifouling were then removed and when the moisture meter was run down these bands (in deep reading mode), the point at which the hull construction changed could easily be identified by a substantial drop in the moisture levels where the laminate changed from sandwich to solid construction

Correlation between readings in both deep and shallow mode strongly suggests that the moisture detected was within the foam core material.

It is thus my opinion without the benefit of further destructive testing that significant and potentially harmful levels of moisture are present in the foam core in the area approximately 7'6" x 20" on the stb side as described above. The presence of this moisture may lead to delamination and degrading of the core material, both of which are serious structural defects but is not possible to place a time scale on any deterioration. The hammer sounding did not suggest any delamination or serious deterioration to the core but this may be present in its early stages but not yet detectable by the non destructive methods available during this survey. There are differing opinions as to how serious moisture ingress to foam cores used in this type of construction should be taken but in my experience this is potentially a very serious defect.

Right at the forward end of the area described above there is a slight depression in the hull with a diameter of about 12". This is most likely due to a cradle support having borne too much weight during a period laid up ashore, this having distorted the hull. However there is no clear indication here of any delamination or significant structural defect.

Delamination of balsa cored hull

All of the topsides and most of the underbody are of FRP sandwich type construction with an end grain balsa core. Light hammer sounding of the hull identified four areas of about 12" diameter where the outer solid FRP laminate is not well bonded to the balsa core, these located as follows:

- Port side aft of amidships about 10" below and 6" aft of the galley sink discharge skin fitting.

- Stb side amidships in three areas about 10" below the waterline. One of these is located just aft of the position of the amidships mooring cleat on deck and the other two just forward of this position.

(All above marked in chalk on the hull). In these four areas the outer FRP laminate could easily be deflected inwards and delamination is clearly present. While the delamination identified can be repaired I cannot say with confidence that further delamination will not occur elsewhere in the future and my advice would be to withdraw from the purchase.

Weakened hull due to defective osmosis treatment

(This extract relates to the boat described and illustrated on page 56)
The boat is described as having had an epoxy treatment four years ago but no further details of this were available. On the port bow crazing was noted in the surface of the epoxy coating, this

corresponding to the position of the water tank bulkhead inside the boat. Crazing at this point is quite common and is due to the hull flexing either side of the hard spot created by the bulkhead. There is a further band of crazing running aft from this to the heads inlet and outlet skin fittings, and of a similar nature running along the hard spot where the base of the moulded berth front is in contact with the hull. Further crazing is also present around both the skin fittings to the extent that the epoxy coating is becoming detached around the discharge fitting. A further band of horizontal crazing running forward from the water tank bulkhead is of most concern as the hull is flexing here to an unacceptable degree and at the point marked with a cross can readily be deflected with very little pressure. The degree of flexure present is more than in the corresponding position on the stb side and considerably more than on other examples of this class previously surveyed.

Light hammer sounding of the hull revealed more variation of tone than one would normally expect, although this did not suggest delamination, more the possibility of variation in hull thickness. Various localised areas were also identified that were a good deal more flexible than one would expect.

It was noted that the original gelcoat has been left in place around the heads skin fittings (see Fig 40).

This shows the discharge and the white area is the original gelcoat. A fillet of epoxy filler was in place around the gelcoat edge but when this was removed a clear step between the edge of the original gelcoat and the surface of the new epoxy coating was visible, i.e. a good deal more material has been removed in this area than has been put back.

A similar effect was noted around the galley sink discharge. Here the gelcoat has not been left in situ but there is a 5mm gap between the underside of the skin fitting and the surface of the epoxy coating. I can see no reason why the underside of the skin fitting should not be lying tight and fair to the hull surface and again it would appear that a good deal more material was removed around this fitting than was put back. The above observations suggest that not only has the gelcoat been removed as part of the osmosis treatment but that some of the hull laminate has also been lost. In severe cases of osmosis some delamination and interlaminar blistering becomes apparent when the gelcoat is removed and re-lamination of the underbody is required to restore the original strength but that does not appear to have been carried out. It is also possible that the gelcoat was removed by shot blasting or grinding and that this has been far too aggressive, resulting in some loss of laminate.

It is not possible to be certain as to the exact nature and extent of the problem without extensive destructive testing which of course is not possible without the owner's consent. What is beyond any doubt however is that the underbody is flexing to an unacceptable degree in a number of places, most seriously on the port bow. Given the impossibility of establishing the extent of the problem at this stage it would therefore be my advice to withdraw from the purchase.

Distortion in uncured hull

The hull is of straight FRP construction utilising chopped strand matt and some woven rovings.

No sign of major impact or repair evident through the antifouling or where this was removed. No stress crazing evident around root of keels or skeg. Light hammer sounding (not heavy enough to damage the gelcoat) did not suggest any delamination or other serious laminate defects.

At the aft end of both bilge keels there are distinct hollows in the hull. However with my full weight swinging on the transom of the boat no further distortion was noted. These hollows are almost certainly the result of the boat being taken out of the mould in a 'green' state, i.e. not fully cured. The boat would then have been stood on her bilge keels and her own weight would have caused the distortion which then became permanent as the hull fully cured. However there would have been no loss of structural strength.

Advanced wicking (This extract relates to the hull illustrated in Fig 32)

Vessel was found with some build up of old antifouling and this was removed at random in 22 areas approx. 150mm x 70mm, to reveal the original unpigmented (clear) gelcoat. In all of the areas where gelcoat was exposed wicking was noted, this generally more prominent on the port side. Wicking is the take up of moisture by capillary action. What appear as single filaments of glass are in fact composed of microscopic strands bundled together. Moisture permeates through the gelcoat and is taken up by these bundles as a result of capillary action and they eventually swell, breaking away from the surrounding resin, and the condition becomes visible to the naked eye. Wicking is not an osmotic process, but is often the precursor to osmotic blistering. In this case the wicking is quite advanced, and embryonic blisters are beginning to form, typically where a number of the fibre bundles intersect. A few of these were opened up and found to contain a trace of liquid, but this not yet under pressure as in a true osmotic blister.

Moisture readings over all the areas where antifouling was removed were high and consistent with the advanced wicking described above. High moisture content and wicking such as this are not serious structural defects except in rare cases where the laminate is of poor quality or very thin.

In this case it is almost inevitable that osmotic blistering will become evident in the next couple of years and that full remedial treatment will be required.

Note: Occasionally when a hull is treated for osmosis more extensive laminate damage is found which requires re-laminating. This is unusual and the hammer sounding of this hull does not suggest any delamination etc to be present but it is not possible to be 100% sure until the gelcoat is removed as part of the treatment.

This is a substantially built hull and it is not unsound. However in order to preserve the boat's value and to avoid the long term risk of more serious laminate damage it would be prudent to include the cost of osmosis treatment in the next two years' projected maintenance costs.

Aeration of the gelcoat

Vessel was found with quite a heavy and uneven build up of old antifouling in place and this is becoming flaky in places. However no action is required other than to remove any loose material with a wire brush or scraper prior to overcoating with new.

The antifouling was removed at random in 30 areas approx 70mm x 70mm for inspection of the underlying surface and recording of moisture readings. In 15% of those areas localised aeration of the gelcoat was noted. Aeration of the gelcoat is caused by tiny air bubbles being trapped in the gelcoat when it was originally painted onto the mould surface. The condition is very common on older examples of this design and provided the boat is wintered ashore to allow some natural drying out to occur it causes no problem.

Moisture readings were taken in the areas where the antifouling was removed using a capacitance type moisture meter of Sovereign Quantum type, operating in both shallow and deep reading modes. The meter was first checked for correct calibration. The readings recorded below are from the meter operating in the shallow mode on the relative scale 0–100. When switched to deep reading mode there was no appreciable increase in the readings and this confirms that no further deep seated moisture is present.

The readings are relative and do not express moisture content as a percentage of dry weight. High moisture content is not generally a structural defect, and is to be expected in older boats. However where some moisture has been absorbed the likelihood of moisture related problems occurring is higher, and the actual state of the laminate cannot be completely guaranteed without destructive testing followed by chemical analysis. The opinion given in this survey is based on all the evidence available at the time but without destructive testing.

The conditions prevailing when the readings were taken were as follows:

METER	RANGE BELOW WATERLINE	RANGE ABOVE WATERLINE
Sovereign Quantum, Scale A, 0–100	13–16	12–13
Deep Mode	No significant increase	No significant increase

The values recorded below the waterline are very low and very close to the values recorded above the waterline on parts of the hull that have rarely been immersed. Laminate considered to be in satisfactory condition at this time. With older boats moulded with the type of resins as used here, always storing the vessel ashore out of season to allow some natural drying out to occur is recommended. In this case the aeration of the gelcoat identified is allowing moisture to permeate the laminate but it is drying out during the periods stored ashore. It is thus important that the established pattern of wintering ashore is maintained.

Bodged osmosis treatment

Owner states that the vessel had the gelcoat removed and replaced with an epoxy coating in the spring of this year but no invoice was available. However the Owner states no osmotic blistering was present, he merely wished to renew the underwater surface in the light of the boat's age.

However in the trailing edge of the skeg (an area shaped to fit the profile of the rudder leading edge and not accessible for repair without removing the rudder), numerous craters and voids were noted. These have the appearance of past blisters which have broken out and simply been over coated with antifouling. Owner states that the epoxy coating is covered by a guarantee, and that would normally be the case. However no supporting documentation was supplied, and such a guarantee is not specified in the contract as one of the documents being delivered to the purchaser on completion.

It is therefore necessary to establish the following:

- Is the work guaranteed and for what period.
- Is any guarantee transferable to a new owner (as is usually the case upon payment of a small fee within a set period, normally within 30 days of completion).

- If any work becomes necessary within the guarantee period, then can this be carried out at a location convenient to the new Owner, and under the supervision of an independent surveyor (all costs to be covered by the guarantee).

The moisture readings recorded below the waterline were all very high and warrant further investigation. (After only one season afloat since osmosis treatment the readings on the underbody would normally be virtually identical to those recorded above the waterline.) Only three reasons for such high readings are possible:

- The laminate was not dried out properly prior to the application of the epoxy coatings.
- The material applied contains metallic compounds which are causing spurious readings. Some epoxy paints and fillers do contain such compounds, typically zinc or zinc phosphate, and are widely used as protective coatings on mild steel. In my experience however the materials normally used in an osmosis treatment do not have a significant influence upon capacitance type moisture meters, and such effect is known and quantified.

- One or more of the coatings applied have not cured properly and have absorbed moisture.

The shipyard have described the coatings applied as follows:

Four coats of conventional epoxy resin. A final heavy coat described as having 'active corrosion protection in a layer consisting of iron mica and zinc plates', and they further state that the presence of this material would cause high moisture readings without the presence of abnormal moisture within the laminate. This material may be Barrier Coat 422 as supplied by West Systems. It is widely used and is designed to improve moisture exclusion and combat osmosis. However its presence has little effect on capacitance type meters, and such effect is known and quantified.

During the survey I also carried out the following routine procedures which do not support the proposition that the coatings are the cause of the high readings:

- In one area forward on the port side the final 'heavy coat' as described above was scraped away to reveal the underlying epoxy resin. Readings taken on this surface were identical to those taken prior to removal.
- All the new coatings have been taken a few cms above the waterline, this being normal good practice. Moisture readings were taken on the epoxy surface right at its top edge and these were found to be very low. In these positions above the static waterline where the hull is not normally immersed one would expect to find low moisture levels and that was the case, even with the epoxy materials in place. However the readings increase dramatically as the meter is moved below the waterline.

Small blisters between 3–5mm in diameter were also noted in the epoxy surface, these sparse but well distributed over the underbody. A few were opened up at random and appeared to be at the interface of the last two coats of epoxy. A further inspection was undertaken using a very powerful spotlight beam to throw any further embryonic blisters into relief and more were identified. Such blistering within the coating after only a few months is cause for serious concern and obviously seriously prejudices its effectiveness. It can have various causes but is commonly seen where the underlying laminate is not sufficiently dry and also when incomplete cure is present.

To summarise:

- The foregoing is the limit which can be achieved without extensive destructive testing.
- Osmosis is only one symptom of high moisture content and it is this that must be lowered before any treatment can be successful and lasting.
- The procedures I have carried out without destructive testing suggest the high moisture content to be within the hull laminate. However it is accepted that the coatings may contain compounds that grossly affect the readings, although I have never encountered this before. It is also possible one or more of the coatings have only partially cured or have broken down.
- The presence of the intercoat blistering after only a few months is in any case a serious defect which must be rectified and accounted for.

Recommendation: Small sample areas of the epoxy coatings should be progressively removed down to the laminate with moisture readings taken in stages to verify where any moisture is located. If it is established that the hull laminate is not dry the entire treatment should be carried out again after proper steam washing and drying of the laminate. The intercoat blistering is a serious defect and must in any case be rectified and explained.

Background

Since the original survey the vessel has been moved into the workshop for remedial work to the epoxy treatment, this under warranty. I initially inspected the workshops and equipment of the above yard and found the premises to be well equipped and organised. I am thus now satisfied this business is capable of carrying out work to a good standard.

Observations

The boat was seen with the epoxy coatings stripped off revealing the original gelcoat surface. It is now clear that the vessel has not undergone a full epoxy treatment as originally stated by the owner. The gelcoat had been pitted to allow a path for moisture to escape, and also significantly reduced in thickness. In numerous places various voids had been merely filled, this particularly so on the stb side. Elsewhere in small areas the gelcoat had been removed entirely and some wicking could be seen in the laminate. Wicking is the take up of moisture by capillary action. What appear as single filaments of glass are in fact composed of microscopic strands bundled together. Moisture permeates through the gelcoat and is taken up by these bundles as a result of the capillary action, and they eventually swell causing the gelcoat to be raised slightly and the condition becomes visible to the naked eye. The voids referred to above (now filled) are most likely embryonic blisters which were beginning to form, typically where a number of the fibre bundles intersect. This is a common condition and is usually the precursor of true osmotic blistering.

Recommendations: The owner proposes simply re-coating the boat as before. However this is entirely unsatisfactory for the following reasons:

- When moisture has been present in a typical FRP laminate over a long period, various residual solvents etc within it become active. An essential part of any treatment is to open up the laminate surface to allow flushing out of this material, returning the laminate as far as possible to an inert state. Obviously this cannot be achieved with the gelcoat in place.

- Although a significant fall in moisture levels was noted it will be extremely difficult to achieve recommended dryness with the gelcoat in place and most certainly not in the timescale proposed. Achieving recommended dryness is again essential to the success of the treatment.

It is thus considered essential to proceed as per a full osmosis treatment involving total removal of the gelcoat, intensive washing and then drying down to recommended levels. It is significant to note that the shipyard is only prepared to offer 12 months warranty if the vessel is simply re-coated, while they will offer seven years for a full treatment. As described in my original report it would be prudent to ensure that the terms of any warranty are acceptable.

Crazing to hull

Some localised stress crazing was noted at the following points:

- Stb side just below the waterline between the position of the cap shroud and aft lower shroud there is longitudinal crazing over about 600mm.
- 600mm aft from the above crazing some further limited longitudinal crazing is present.
- The above has been caused by the hull flexing either side of a hard spot caused by a longitudinal plywood stiffener bonded into the hull outboard of the berth.
- Stb side of keel root from leading edge running aft.

All of the above crazing appears to be relatively minor, that is confined to the gelcoat and not extending into the laminate. However this can only be completely verified by grinding out sample areas of the gelcoat for full inspection and it is suggested this be undertaken as convenient. The crazing was very difficult to identify, in fact the first area was found by chance in the process of removing antifouling for taking moisture readings. The remaining area of the hull was examined repeatedly during the survey under changing light conditions and no further crazing was evident showing through the antifouling. However given that this boat has completed two Caribbean circuits in recent years it would be unusual if no further crazing was present hidden under the thick antifouling and epoxy coating but any that was serious enough to significantly weaken the laminate and cause it to flex would be visible through the coatings (which have clearly not been recently applied).

The best course of action would be to have the existing antifouling and epoxy coatings removed to allow full examination of the hull. However, based on the evidence available at time of survey it is my opinion that no very serious structural defect would be revealed, but this cannot be guaranteed without full removal of the coatings and subsequent examination. Moisture readings over the crazing were not significantly higher than elsewhere and it is suggested the crazed areas identified be stripped back to the gelcoat and epoxy painted using one of the proprietary preventative epoxy paints to prevent moisture ingress.

● SECTION 4, TOPSIDES ABOVE WATERLINE INCLUDING RUBBING STRAKE ETC.

- Establish type of construction.
- Original gelcoat or paint coating? Check around fittings, up under any rubbing strake etc. In particular beware part painted topsides, is this a major repair? Immediately look inside the vessel at the corresponding area.
- Cosmetic condition, UV degrading?
- Any crazing, particularly around hard spots? If you find serious crazing if possible test the hull for stiffness at that point compared with the corresponding area on the other side.
- Where tie rods or figs attach to knees etc bonded into the topsides, check the topsides externally for distortion.
- Abrasion damage?
- Hammer sound for voids or delamination.
- Rubbing strake condition and security? Are its fastenings also those of the hull/deck join?

REPORT EXTRACTS

General topside wear and tear plus saturated laminate

Topsides found reasonably fair and finished in the original gelcoat. The gelcoat surface is somewhat worn and UV degraded but not yet at the stage where painting is required.
There is a good deal of general chafe damage, chipping and scratching present commensurate with age but with some gelcoat filling, compound polishing and waxing a good cosmetic appearance could be restored. There is some general gelcoat impact crazing on the port bow outboard over about 2 sq ft, but this is not extending into the laminate. Moisture readings over the crazing satisfactory and a good coat of wax polish will inhibit any future ingress.

There is a band of vertical crazing aft of amidships on the port hull outboard where flexing has taken place either side of a bulkhead. The hull here is no more flexible than elsewhere and it is considered unlikely any laminate damage is present.

Some previous damage to the transom to stb of the centreline has been roughly repaired but this basically sound under hammer testing.

On the port quarter just above the chine an area of the laminate sounds very hollow and when a spike was driven into this area water streamed out. This area is about 6ft x 6ft and also extending round onto the base of the transom.

Moisture readings taken working away from the saturated area suggest this ingress is as a result of water entering various damaged areas of gelcoat above the waterline, or around the exhaust fitting which is not lying tight to the transom, which is also crazed due to impact.

Recommendation: The area of the topside laminate which is saturated and degraded at the port quarter should be ground out, dried and re-laminated. The source of the ingress should also be established and attended to.

Delaminated topsides

Topside moulding found very fair and finished in blue paint applied over the original gelcoat. It is clear that the original gelcoat surface was much UV degraded prior to being painted and the cracked surface can be seen through the paint in places, this most pronounced on the transom. The paint coating is in reasonable condition and is quite smart from a few feet away.

The topsides have been repaired port and stb at the bow and in various other places and hammer sounding of these areas was satisfactory.

On the starboard side the topsides are flexing to an alarming degree from the aftermost chain plate running aft to the position of stanchion 2. In this area the laminate can easily be deflected by light pressure. It was not possible to examine this area from inside the boat due to the fixed inner moulding. The port topside was found to be good and stiff in the corresponding area as was the rest of the topsides.

There is also some heavy crazing and possible laminate damage in this area where the hull has flexed either side of a hard spot created by bulkheads and other partitions inside the boat. The worst of this is about amidships on the stb side and this area has also absorbed large amounts of moisture and is thus longstanding damage.

This is a design that has achieved a good reputation for serious offshore use and it is somewhat surprising to encounter such flexing. It is considered most likely that the vessel has endured a very long offshore leg on port tack in extreme conditions whereby the stb topsides have been pounded over a long period and some delamination has occurred. It is also possible that for one reason or another this example was not as heavily built as she should have been. In her present condition the vessel is only suitable for coastal use due to the weak topsides and it will be necessary to strip out the inner moulding to ascertain why this has happened and how to repair the laminate.

Recommendation: The topsides are flexing to an unacceptable degree in the area from the aftermost chain plate starboard side aft to stanchion 2 and the inner moulding should be removed to allow full inspection and repair.

● SECTION 5, DECK MOULDING

- Establish type of construction. Most production yachts have balsa or foam cored decks. If so, run a moisture meter over all cored areas to identify any ingress (weather permitting). If the deck is wet and this test cannot be carried out SAY SO in report. Be particularly suspicious of ingress around any fittings attached after the boat was built. Look for crushing of the core material under the tension of bolts, this evident as a slight depression around the fitting.

- If deck is of sandwich construction try to get some moisture readings inside the boat on the deckhead, particularly if the deck has a screw fastened teak overlay. Look for places inside the boat where you can see the construction, often visible as a step in the moulding towards the deck edge where it changes from sandwich to solid at the hull/deck joint. Look for through deck fittings such as hawse pipes, ventilators where you can sometimes see the raw edge of the deck or unscrew a trim to expose it.
- Light hammer sound deck and go over it bouncing on tiptoe listening for a crackling and crunching sound which often indicates the early stages of delamination. Also feel for any flexing and give during this test. If, as is often the case, you start the survey afloat then continue after lifting do this test with the boat ashore because when she is afloat and can move in the water this test bouncing on tiptoe is nowhere near as effective. This is most important.
- Cosmetic condition?
- Any damage, stress crazing?
- Any distortion or crazing in way of load bearing fittings?
- If mast stepped on deck, aggressively swig (ie pull out line, thus increasing tension) the shrouds to check for any movement at the mast step (smaller boats).
- Does deck have a teak overlay? Condition and possibility of seepage into the balsa core if screw fastenings are used. Note some production boats have a 'teak' deck which is merely teak veneer on plywood. This can be identified by staggered joints every 8ft or so. Ingress to the core material can be a hugely expensive defect to rectify so spend some time on this.

REPORT EXTRACTS

Delaminating and sodden balsa cored deck

Internally there is very little access to the deckhead due to fixed linings but as far as I can ascertain the deck is mainly solid FRP with beam stiffening but with some areas of balsa sandwich construction.

There is an unacceptable degree of flexing in the foredeck stb side and also running aft along the stb sidedeck to the main rigging U-bolts. This bears all the signs of being a balsa sandwich construction which has delaminated. Moisture readings here are also very high in places suggesting ingress to the core material. It will be necessary to strip out the linings to establish the exact construction of the deck here but repairs are considered essential.

Very worn teak veneer deck and possible ingress to balsa core

The deck is of FRP sandwich construction with end grain balsa core stiffening. Plywood is incorporated into the laminate in way of load bearing fittings and areas of high stress. Deck found firm underfoot with no sign of delamination or other structural defect.

All the horizontal surfaces have been covered with a teak veneered plywood giving the appearance of a laid and swept teak deck. The material is generally adhering well enough but is very badly worn, split and also delaminating in places. The cosmetic appearance is very poor.

Four of the teak plugs covering the screw holes were removed at random around the deck and no screws were found in situ. As far as I can ascertain the screws were used to hold the plywood in place while the adhesive/sealant upon which it was laid cured, and the screws were then removed.

This leaves a series of holes in the top FRP lamination which provide a potential path for moisture into the balsa core material. These should all be filled but are frequently not.

Based on previous experience I would expect that some ingress to the core material is present but given that the plywood is well bedded on adhesive/sealant this is most likely to be localised and minor at this stage. (Due to the extensive linings it was not possible to obtain any moisture readings on the deckhead inside the boat and to be absolutely sure as to moisture ingress it would be necessary to remove all the linings).

However, given the fact that the plywood is now in poor condition and that it is freely absorbing moisture it would be unwise to leave the deck in this condition as the moisture will increasingly creep under the sealant.

Clearly replacing the deck will be a major expense. Practically every deck fitting will have to be removed, and removal of the plywood and adhesive will be very difficult. Some saving could be made by using Treadmaster material in lieu of the teak, perhaps with a teak covering board along the deck edge. Obviously given the cost it would be sensible to obtain quotations prior to purchase.

> Always be prepared for the unexpected!

Most of the horizontal surfaces are covered in a thick layer of blue deck paint, this being the standard finish from new. Virtually all the painted areas were seen to be blistering. Further investigation revealed these blisters to be not within the paint coatings, but at the interface of the gelcoat and laminate. Several blisters were opened up at random and were found to contain fluid under pressure. The fluid was tested and found to be acidic, with a ph of 7. The majority of the blisters were between 10 and 20mm in diameter, and extended examination under changing light conditions revealed them to be widespread throughout the painted deck areas.

Recommendation: The type of blistering present in the superstructure is very unusual and I have not previously encountered it to such an advanced extent. I can only assume that the thick build up of deck paint has retained moisture to a sufficient degree to trigger and maintain the osmotic process, this accelerated by an abnormal degree of solvent retention or similar in the laminate. In this area we have had eight consecutive months where rainfall has broken the record for each particular month, and the level in the last year is 3 times the annual average. Thus the deck would have been continuously wet for months at a time but it is still surprising that this level of osmosis has occurred. It is likely there are other factors partly responsible, such as solvent entrapment within the original laminate, but if this was the case one would expect to find some defects within the white non painted areas, but that was not the case.

The deck is still considered of adequate strength but it would not be prudent to leave the blisters too long because the acidic liquid therein will permeate deeper into the laminate and has the potential to cause more serious harm. It is therefore suggested that the gelcoat be ground out in the affected areas and the laminate thoroughly hot pressure washed to flush out acidic residues and other free agents. Thorough drying out will then be necessary prior to re-coating the laminate and it may be found that the Hot Vac system will be the most effective in achieving this. The deck should then be faired in the conventional manner and epoxy coated. However given the poor UV resistance of epoxies the final coatings should be of two pack polyurethane. It is suggested fine non slip compound be mixed with this to provide a long lasting non slip finish. (Given that all the areas affected are non slip painted it will not be necessary to provide a very smooth faired finish and there will be some saving in costs in this respect.)

● SECTION 6, COACHROOF

- Basically same criteria as previous section, plus:
- Any distortion or crazing under mast step? If yes examine the support for the mast compression inside the boat and in particular if twin keel examine the hull externally for any distortion at the base of the compression post, bulkhead etc.
- Handrails secure.
- If mast stepped on coachroof or deck aggressively swig the shrouds to check of any movement at the mast step (smaller boats).

REPORT EXTRACT

Deflection in coachroof under mast step

Some deflection is present to the coachroof under the mast step and further reference is made to this in section 9 below. (This is best seen kneeling on the foredeck looking aft).

Mast compression is transferred to the hull via a compression post immediately under the mast step, this landed on a structural frame (termed a floor by designers and boatbuilders) moulded integrally with the inner moulding. One would normally expect this to be a solid frame and it is positioned over the end of the keel so cannot flex or crush to any great degree.

However, as described in section 7 above some distortion to the coachroof was noted in way of the mast step, and some deflection is also taking place to this structural frame at the base of the compression post. Here the deflection is 8mm measured from a straight edge laid across the frame immediately forward of the post, thus it would appear that this frame is not packed out solid but is hollow. Some deflection is often seen which is due to initial crushing of materials having occurred early in a yacht's life and then ceased but the degree seen here requires further investigation.

Recommendation: Given the deflection seen in the coachroof and box section structural frame (floor) at the base of the mast compression post the linings at the top of the mast compression post should be removed in order that the top of the post and coachroof deck head can be fully inspected. It will also be necessary to cut into the box section structural floor under the base of the post to determine its construction.

● SECTION 7, COCKPIT

- Structural and cosmetic assessment as for deck and coachroof.
- In particular look for delamination in sole (high traffic area).
- Is cockpit self draining, are all locker lids, sole panels etc secure with efficient gaskets?
- Condition of any slats and gratings? Take up any gratings etc and test the sole for delamination, any gratings etc may have been put in because of this.
- Security and condition of any wheel pedestal and crash bar.

REPORT EXTRACT

Delaminated cockpit sole

Integral with deck moulding and of self draining type. Deep locker located to stb. Lid securely hinged with positive method of closure. There are no lifting sole panels giving access to engine etc. and as such this is a genuine self draining cockpit with good high bridgedeck.

There is extensive delamination to the cockpit sole which is of sandwich construction. This may be rectified by screwing longitudinal hardwood battens about 3/8" x 2" onto the sole using self tapping screws, with the battens also bonded in place with epoxy adhesive. A gap of about 1" should be left between the battens which can be oiled to create a good appearance.

The last three sections, i.e. Deck, Coachroof and Cockpit, are usually the same moulding and in addition to the structural issues already discussed are subject to the same cosmetic deterioration throughout the moulding. High traffic areas are obviously more prone to wear and this is important to remember with a teak overlay. With all types of deck the point in the side decks where you tread getting out of the cockpit is probably the most prone to wear, or even delamination in a cored deck, particularly if it involves a sort of jump over the coaming and landing on one leg or similar. Cockpit seat tops and soles are equally vulnerable.

The entire moulding will suffer the same kind of cosmetic damage, the most common being crazing, wear, and UV degrading of the surface. All are merely cosmetic, unless any crazing is accompanied by laminate fracturing which should be obvious. Crazing either side of a hard spot such as a moulded beam or a bulkhead in a solid laminate (as illustrated in Fig 14) is also common. It is important to use a moisture meter over crazed areas to identify any ingress, and provided it is just crazing no action is usually essential, and I usually give the advice that a thick coat of wax polish applied regularly will inhibit moisture ingress. Of course the crazing can be ground out and repaired but to get a good colour match on old gelcoat can reduce the most skilled craftsmen to tears.

On the subject of FRP repairs, take time to download the excellent free manuals from West Systems, **www.westsystem.com/ss/use-guides/**. These contain a wealth of information about FRP construction and repair methods.

The crazing in Fig 45 is confined to the gelcoat and not extending into the laminate. It is very common indeed because the stanchion is just a long lever attached to the deck and often subject to shock

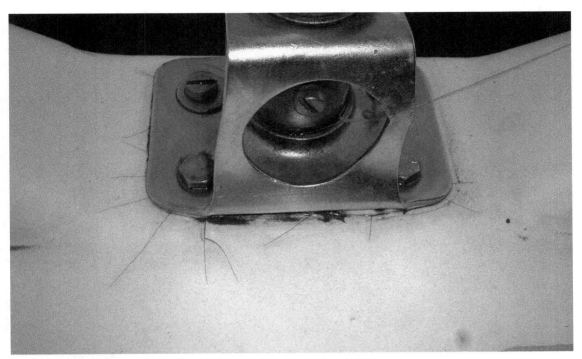

Fig 45: Typical crazing around stanchion base.

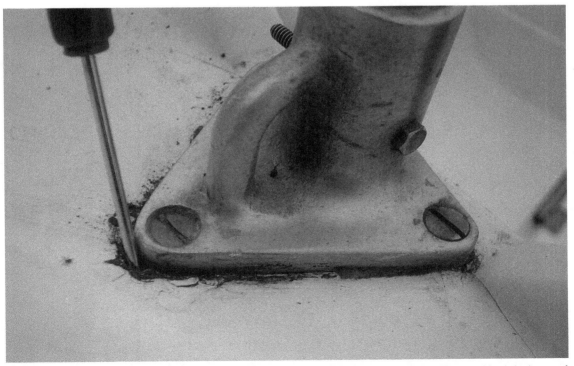

Fig 46: Damaged deck. In this case the laminate is clearly fractured and requires structural repair. The stanchion is in danger of being ripped out of the deck if loaded.

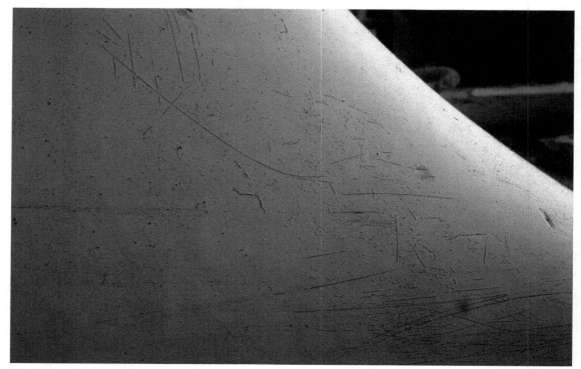

Fig 47: Minor UV degrading of gelcoat surface.

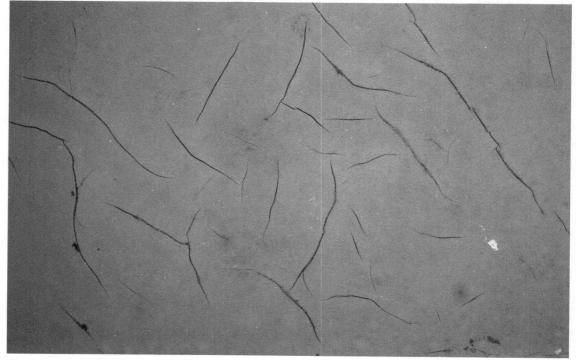

Fig 48: Severe UV degrading.

loading as people fall against it or grab it. In this case the impact has been sufficient to distort a very strong stainless steel base unit but the deck is structurally intact, this easily confirmed by testing the stiffness here (using the convenient lever) with the stiffness of the corresponding area on the other side of the boat. In fact it is standard procedure whenever a comparison is required to test the same part of the boat on the other side, and this is just another small test and observation that moves opinion closer to fact. The same holds true for structural damage – always be thinking how any impact may travel through the structure and damage areas away from the impact, typically opposite.

Do not confuse crazing with UV degrading. In Fig 47 the UV degrading has the appearance of tiny pinholes and crevices in the surface. In Fig 48 the condition is much more severe with actual cracks. Both conditions are made much more unsightly by dirt collecting in the crevices. Both are cosmetic defects only.

● SECTION 8, HULL/DECK JOIN

- Establish type. This is either mechanical using bolts and/or rivets, or FRP bonded and overlaminated. Mechanical types usually have flanges inboard but some will use external flanges visible outside the boat. These are particularly vulnerable to damage. Most flange type joints have an aluminium toerail which utilises the same bolts. Check the toerail for any damage and distortion which may have strained the joint.
- Check for any movement, leaks or evidence of same where not accessible (stains on linings etc, use moisture meter).
- If of bolted type with aluminium toerail (very common), check condition of toerail where stainless steel bolts pass through, serious corrosion to the aluminium in way of the bolts is common on older boats.
- Check toerail for distortion due to impact, may cause joint to leak.
- It is common to find rubbing strakes attached with ferrous bolts through FRP bonded joints. This does not usually affect integrity of joint but may leak as bolts rust away.
- Some bolted joints have stainless steel nuts and bolts but mild steel washers. As the washers rust tension is lost on the bolts and joint may leak.

REPORT EXTRACT

Possible leaking hull/deck join

This is of mechanical type through bolted and also FRP overlaminated apart from across the transom. It was noted that the plywood lining panel at the hull/deck join in the aft cabin was buckled and bowed, suggesting it has been wet. Readings with a moisture meter confirmed a good deal of moisture within the adjacent plywood and right aft in this cabin there are numerous water stains on the fabric lining immediately beneath the plywood panel. In this vicinity are the pushpit plus aft mooring cleat (both through bolted) and these would appear to be leaking. The toerail then runs forward and this may be the source of further seepage. Similar buckling and dampness to the corresponding plywood panels was noted in the forecabin both port and stb. It is considered likely that the toerail fastenings are not bolts but large self tapping screws which have come right through the FRP, providing a potential source of leaks.

● SECTION 9, BULKHEADS AND STRUCTURAL STIFFENING INCLUDING INTERNAL MOULDINGS

- Check all bonding of plywood bulkheads and partitions. With teak faced bulkheads check that teak veneer has been removed prior to bonding in because if the bond is made to the oily teak veneer it will inevitably fail. Occasionally entire boats will be encountered fitted out in this manner and rectification is extremely expensive.

- Hammer sound and discreetly spike test plywood components where moisture ingress is likely, i.e. in bilges or where through deck chain figs are bolted to bulkheads. Take general moisture readings on areas which should have remained basically dry. Beware of sinkers! If widespread unexplained high readings are found the boat has probably been sunk in the past. (Look for replaced headlinings, upholstery etc.) Where a boat has been flooded the plywood bulkheads will remain damp and probably rot, particularly behind the FRP bondings. Take extra care with sounding on formica covered bulkheads.

- With a sailing yacht establish how the mast compression loadings are transferred from the deck/coachroof into the structure, typically by a bulkhead or separate compression post. Is there any movement, distortion, fracturing etc at the base of the bulkhead or post? Is there any distortion, crazing etc around the step externally? Obviously with fin keelers the bulkhead or post will be landed on the keel but beware bilge keelers particularly where a compression post is simply landed on

Fig 49: Testing for failing bonding.

the hull which may be of insufficient strength. Look for distortion, crazing and fracturing along the centreline under the boat where the post is located.

- Check all reinforcing bonded into hull, i.e. frames and stringers. These are commonly formed over plywood or hardwood that is fully encapsulated but then pierced by limber holes, allowing the timber to soak up moisture and rot. So where possible get a spike into the limber holes. (These should be sealed with flowcoat inside but are frequently not.)
- Check bonding of any inner mouldings as much as possible.
- Check all components for any movement or stress cracks, particularly over keel root and at base of mast or compression post.
- Many modern boats have frames etc incorporated into the inner moulding which is then bonded to the hull and considerable structural strength is lost if the mouldings part company. Lightly sound the moulding wherever it should be bonded to the hull moulding and report any voids etc which suggest it is not bonded.
- Where bulkheads locate in a recess within the inner moulding check for any serious movement or displacement of mastic etc. Do all the doors fit and close properly?

Figs 51 and 52 show the result of a light pounding on an east coast sandbank. The repair here was major and just about every reinforcing member in way of the twin keels had to be rebuilt.

Fig 50: Rotting compression post. Water from bilges travelling up end grain and rotting post.

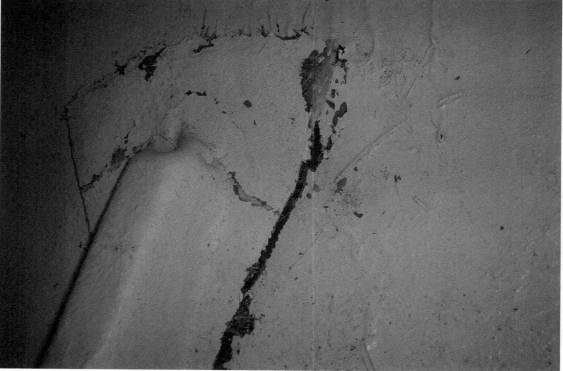

Figs 51 and 52: Structural damage to keel reinforcing.

REPORT EXTRACTS

Inadequate mizzen mast support

There is significant distortion to the deck in way of the mizzen mast step and the moulding is also fractured just forward of the helm seat, this associated with the mast compression. It was noted that there is no support directly under the mast step and severe distortion is also visible from inside the boat. Whilethe vessel has lived with this since building the time has come to improve the support as the possibility of catastrophic failure now exists. In a seagoing ketch (as this boat is) the mizzen will be used in extreme conditions.

Recommendation: It is suggested a simple stainless steel compression post be fitted directly under the mizzen step in the aft cabin. This will not interfere unduly with the accommodation arrangements. For the delivery trip a temporary support such as an Acrow or timber support may be fixed in place.

Repairs to twin keeler in way of mast compression post

The mainmast compression loadings are transferred from the coachroof to hull via a stainless steel compression post. The hull has recently been reinforced with moulded transverse floors in way of the base and the original adjacent partitions re-bonded. It is believed the compression post has also been replaced due to the original of steel having rusted at the base flange, a common defect in this design.

The above work is to a high standard and the region is now stronger than when new.

Defective bulkhead bonding

A serious problem exists with the bonding of bulkheads and partitions. Virtually all the bonding is failing due to poor initial installation whereby the teak veneer was not first removed from the bulkheads and the oil within the teak has prevented sound adhesion. A similar situation exists within the heads compartment where the bulkhead is faced with formica or similar material and this has not been removed or at least deeply scored to provide a key. The bondings are also on the light side and quite narrow and although this is a contributory factor it is less important, and many yachts of this general type survive well enough in normal use with bonding of this strength.

When repairs are undertaken it is important that the new bonding incorporates 'peel arrestors' whereby the first lamination is the narrowest with subsequent layers increasing in width, thus providing multiple bonds and steps where any subsequent failure will be contained. The bonding should be to a minimum thickness of 6oz and it is considered acceptable to limit the width extending onto the bulkheads to allow re-use of the existing teak trims. However it is emphasised that the full width available under these trims must be utilised in all cases.

The two forward primary bulkheads must be re-bonded as described, but it would be acceptable to repair other minor partitions by through bolting in situ using 6mm stainless steel bolts with suitable 'penny washers' under both the heads and nuts. It is thus suggested that where conventional re-bonding of the minor partitions can be achieved it is undertaken as described, but where access is very limited or major destructive dismantling would be necessary then the through bolting method is used.

Possible rot in bulkheads due to previous sinking

The plywood bulkheads throughout the boat are also showing higher than normal moisture content when measured with a moisture meter and given other physical signs I think it possible that this boat has been accidentally submerged at some time in her life. This is not uncommon but it does create conditions whereby small pockets of rot could be present in the structural bulkheads etc; however I have not found any during this survey apart from within the plywood transverse members as described in section 9. (There is some delamination present in the panel forming the top of the quarter berth box accessible in the cockpit locker but this is not a structural member).

ANYONE FOR WOOD?

In case by now you are thinking what a terrible material FRP is, spare a thought for the Owners of the wooden boats in the next series of pictures. Surveying wooden boats is outside the scope of this book but if you encounter FRP hulls with wooden decks and superstructures, always be on the look out for these defects.

Fungal rot

These are the 'hood ends', where the hull planking meets the stem at the bow. In Fig A, undulations can be seen in the wood under the paint on the port bow. Fig B shows the results of light hammer sounding on the stb bow. The cell structure of the timber has collapsed and it is completely rotten due to attack by fungal rot.

The news is no better further aft where the rot has spread along the cell structure of the timber. In the top plank in Fig C, you can again see the surface has become concave where the cell structure is collapsing under the film of paint. This kind of rot is very serious and difficult to eradicate. This kind of deterioration in timber can be readily identified by hull sounding, just as when looking for delamination and voids in FRP laminates. When the condition is this advanced, the hammer makes a depressing dull sound and may actually penetrate the timber. In less extreme cases a spike is used gently to test the hardness of areas where the hammer indicates there may be deterioration.

All fungal rot in boats is serious and may be divided into 'dry rot' and 'wet rot' types, the most dreaded being *Serpula lacrymans*, or 'common dry rot'. However, some species of wet rot are equally destructive given the right conditions to flourish; usually damp, warm and dark areas that are common in the deck structures of many boats. The spores for these fungi are air and rain borne, and can thus penetrate these structures where deck leaks occur, so you may come across it in FRP hulled boats with timber decks etc.

In Figs A, B and C, a small, long-term deck leak at the stem has accounted for this pretty east coast centreboarder becoming unseaworthy and uneconomic to repair – all in the space of 16 months.

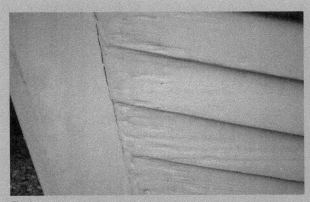

Fig A

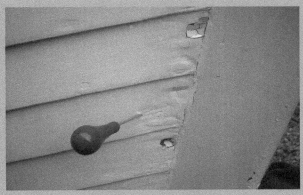

Fig B

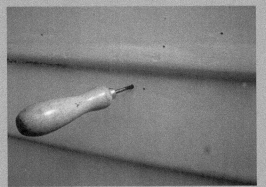

Fig C

Fig D: If you come across this in any boat, be very afraid!

Surveying wooden boats is a highly specialised area, none more so than when dealing with this kind of defect. For those with a suitable background who wish to study this area, there is an excellent book available: *Recognising wood rot and insect damage in buildings* (RICS Books, ISBN 978-1-8608-1603-1). This is a highly illustrated, definitive work in this field. Although primarily written for the building industry, all information is equally relevant to wooden boat structures. If you own a nice classic wooden yacht though don't buy this book - it's not for the faint hearted!

Maybe FRP doesn't seem so bad after all?

Electrochemical decay

This is a common defect in wooden boats. In very simple terms it is a process whereby the timber, in way of the anodic and cathodic ends of a galvanic cell, can turn to pulp due to the exchange of ions taking place. It is commonly seen around bronze stern and rudder tubes where these pass through the centreline structure and often causes leaks here. In Fig E the wood is completely rotten and will probably be the same deep inside this substantial piece of timber. The rudder tube has also become loose and is leaking. In this case there is no alternative other than dismantling the whole assembly for major repair.

Fig E

Fig F

Fig G

Fig H

Another common manifestation of this process is where the timber around the fastenings in hull planking deteriorates, rendering the planks loose and causing leaks. In some parts of the country this is known as 'nail sickness' and is a very serious defect. It is also commonly seen where iron or steel 'strap' floors have been fastened with copper or bronze fastenings. Sometimes the decayed timber can be cut out and a new 'graving piece' let in but in advanced cases re-planking can be necessary.

This type of decay can actually be prompted by applying a cathodic protection system to a vessel which has hitherto never had any serious corrosion problems, and there is often a lack of consensus on these kinds of systems.

Saturation

As described above, FRP boats with wooden decks and superstructures are quite common, and plywood is used extensively in this type of construction. The golden rule here is to look out for any deck leaks, or places where rain water may lodge, because fresh water will often cause serious softening and eventual rot.

In Fig F the iroko cabin coaming is soft where water has lodged behind the window bezel. The timber has become saturated over a long period, and is now soft. This kind of saturation will discolour the wood and is readily seen when the surface is varnished. Here there is no fungal rot, just saturation, and in many cases the timber will harden up to an acceptable degree once it is thoroughly dried and the source of the saturation stopped.

Fig G shows a typical plywood deck fitted to an FRP hull. Externally the ply is epoxy-sheathed but any leaks caused by poor fitting or damage will eventually cause rot in the ply and ends of the deckbeams.

Pay particular attention to the external sheathing, it should be turned down the vertical topsides to seal and protect the edge of the plywood, not simply butted up against a toerail as is often seen.

Modern timber construction

Timber construction has moved on at a spectacular rate in recent years and particularly since the advent of epoxy adhesives and coatings. This new 'Woods' designed catamaran (Fig H and I) is entirely sheathed externally with glass cloth and epoxy resin, and the hulls are similarly sheathed inside. The hulls are constructed of edge glued cedar strip planking which in effect becomes the filling in a sandwich construction, but with far superior mechanical properties to foam or balsa in an FRP structure. This results in an incredibly strong panel which is also very light. The exterior has been finished using a high spec, two-pack polyurethane paint system which is very hard wearing and has excellent adhesion properties. This vessel has more in common with a moulded FRP hull than a traditionally-built timber boat and should last many many years. This kind of construction lends itself well to one-off yacht building and is used to build some of the finest bespoke yachts in the world today.

Years ago, thousands of boats were built with plywood that was sheathed in glass fibre, using ordinary polyester resin. Without constant maintenance many will have succumbed to extensive saturation and associated rot in the plywood. Until epoxies became readily available and modified for this type of use, getting a good bond between any kind of timber and an FRP laminate was very difficult and prone to failure after heavy use.

If you encounter older boats or even just plywood decks constructed like this, be very wary indeed, hammer sound all areas most carefully and inspect internally for any signs of deck leaks.

The decks and central nacelle in this catamaran are constructed of plywood bonded with fillets of epoxy adhesive. There are far fewer mechanical fastenings in this type of construction than would have been the case a few years ago, such is the strength and reliability of modern epoxy bonds to timber.

Fig I

CHAPTER 7: **INSPECTION SECTIONS 10-13**

The next sub heading from the survey report covers sections 10–13.

Steering, stern gear, and skin fittings etc

10. **Rudder and steering**
11. **Stern gear**
12. **Cathodic protection**
13. **Skin fittings and other through hull apertures**

In this area serious but easily avoidable defects are frequently found, these have the potential to cause loss of the vessel and frequently do.

● SECTION 10, RUDDER AND STEERING

In the days of working sail it used to be said that to lose the rudder was to lose the ship and it is worth keeping that in mind.

- Most GRP rudders consist of two moulded halves bonded around a stainless steel stock. Examine blade for any damage, splits or weeps. Use a mirror to examine the top where it is very close to underside of hull.
- Check all metal rudder blades and any other parts carefully for corrosion, particularly any welds.
- Check material of stock, use a magnet on stainless steels. (Generally if it is magnetic it is a poor grade stainless and prone to corrosion inside the rudder tube at the bottom bush.)
- Examine all hangings, bolts and shoes where applicable. Hammer sound fixing bolts.
- Wherever possible lash the tiller (or lock the steering), then apply all your strength to the rudder blade to check for any movement between the stock and blade. Be brutal. If it breaks it was defective anyway.
- Where applicable check security of rudder tube in hull. If not accessible inside the boat SAY SO.
- Condition of tiller and top fittings? Beware common laminated tillers using mahogany and a light timber such as ramin which is not durable and is prone to rot.
- Play in top and bottom bushes?
- Condition and type of wheel steering gear? Leaks to hydraulics? Broken strands in wire cables? Has the right type of wire been used (NOT 1x19, see Fig 121 and description of wire types in section 22 of survey inspections).
- Security of quadrant or stub tiller etc? Helm indicator working?
- If wheel steering, is there provision for an emergency tiller and is this aboard?

Fig 51 shows severe corrosion to the aluminium rudder stock of a yacht only three years old. This kind of unexplained rapid corrosion is seen quite frequently in the marine environment and in my experience is usually the result of the wrong alloy being used in the first place, i.e. a quality control failure, or current leakage from the vessel's system.

Fig 51: Corrosion in aluminium rudder stock.

There is also another reason which is becoming increasingly common and that is the use of copper-rich antifouling coatings bound in water soluble epoxy coatings. These typically contain 66% copper powder, which in such close proximity to aluminium is bound to cause corrosion given the two metals' position in the galvanic series. Dissimilar metals used in the marine environment cause havoc and an understanding of the galvanic series is vital. Much has been written elsewhere on this subject and this should be studied.

The important thing to note here is that once serious corrosion like this has been identified anywhere all the other fittings below the waterline must be examined and tested with the utmost scrutiny. In Fig 51, one can also see that similar corrosion is affecting the base of the rudder tube which is also of aluminium. There was no access to this inside the boat and only the bottom rim can be seen from under the boat. With a little antifouling, weed etc in place this would not be visible, so do be sure to scrape such areas clean and inspect them fully. Without such inspection the rudder alone could be replaced only for the yacht to sink within a few months due to perforation of the rudder tube.

In Fig 52 the nut appeared sound but shattered when hammer tested, revealing the bolt also severely corroded in the thread. Even high grade stainless steel is unreliable anywhere if oxygen is excluded but

Fig 52: Typical corrosion to stainless steel nut and bolt.

moisture is present, i.e. within the thread of a nut and bolt. It is thus so important to test such fastenings with a hammer, screwdriver and spanner. The blade of a screwdriver is placed on the wall of the nut and the screwdriver tapped with a hammer, if the nut is severely corroded it will disintegrate.

Fig 53 shows one of a series of bolts holding the pintles of a transom hung rudder in place on a seagoing yacht. All 'appeared' sound but when hammered as described above the nuts disintegrated. This is just another one of those simple little tests that move mere opinion to stark fact.

As an aside never use that terrible word 'appeared' in a survey report. If all else fails, 'as far as could be ascertained' (without dismantling, destructive testing etc) is far more appropriate.

We digress slightly with Fig 54 but it provides a graphic illustration of corrosion in stainless steel where moisture is present but oxygen is excluded. This folding boarding ladder has had tight fitting clear plastic tubing fitted over the tubes to prevent chafe damage to the gelcoat. This is above the waterline but moisture has seeped behind the plastic tubing causing the corrosion visible as a brown stain. When the tubing was removed the underlying stainless steel tube wall was 50% wasted in places. So much for stainless steel.

Fig 55 shows the kind of nut commonly used in yacht construction. The nut has a nylon collar within it which locks on the threads and prevents the nut from coming loose. However the nylon collar will

Fig 53: You just don't get this kind of
job satisfaction working in a bank!

Fig 54: Corroding stainless
steel boarding ladder.

Fig 55: Self locking nuts.

Fig 56: Another example of typical corrosion to stainless steel nuts in a rudder hanging.

Fig 57: Corroding bolts in rudder hanging.

absorb and retain moisture, which provides the perfect combination for corrosion to occur inside the nut even when used above the waterline. So pay special attention to these, testing them with both hammer and spanner, and if brown staining is issuing from the nut as in Fig 56, either remove it or make a recommendation that all be stripped and checked.

Fig 57 is taken looking up at the underside of a rudder fitting bolted through the base of the skeg on a lifting keel cruising yacht. All the above bolts fell apart when lightly tapped, and the bottom rudder hanging simply fell off. Not only would the vessel lose her rudder when the bolts inevitably failed, but if this happened at sea the three bolt holes would be left leaking in a part of the boat not accessible from inside without cutting away an inner moulding.

So the importance of applying some kind of physical test on such fastenings cannot be emphasised enough. Even if that test is limited (provided of course the limits of the test are clearly defined in the report), it is a thousand times better than doing nothing, or making ridiculous statements like 'the rudder hangings *appeared* sound and secure'. That word again!

Remember to look thoroughly inside the boat where the rudder tube passes through the hull. The bolts securing the rudder tube in Fig 58 are clearly corroding and when the GRP encapsulation was removed the tube wall was also severely corroded (Fig 58).

The split in Fig 59 is quite obvious but always remember to look under fittings like this hood as far as possible. The tiller here is completely rotten just inside the hood fitting. Fig 60 shows a typical split in the

Fig 58: Corroding rudder tube and bolts.

Fig 59: Split tiller.

base of a rudder blade after having been gently prised open. At first the split was not at all obvious but after gentle prising it was found to extend right around the base. Under such circumstances corrosion to the stock and tangs within, and particularly at the welds, is not uncommon. This is another example where a simple little test, i.e. gently driving a blade into what was not obviously a split, will identify a serious defect and is a thousand times better than doing nothing.

In Fig 62, the boat has no emergency tiller arrangement, the weed hatch immediately forward of the rudder tube prevents one sliding over the stub tiller. Note the cable clamp fitting bottom right, these often rust unseen til they break and steering is lost.

Obviously some form of emergency tiller is necessary and its presence aboard should always be verified.

Fig 60: Split rudder blade.

Note how, in Fig 63, the lower of the two cables has jumped off the quadrant due to being too slack. In Fig 64 we can see that it is jamming between the base of the quadrant and the aluminium cable bracket, and the amount of aluminium dust visible suggests failure is not far off. When dismantled the cable was found to be severely damaged where it had been continuously pinched.

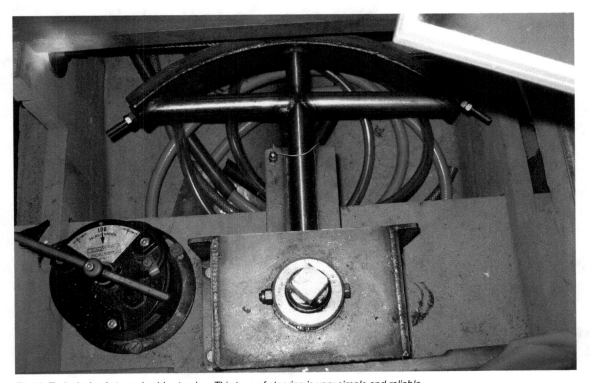

Fig 61: Typical wheel steered cable steering. This type of steering is very simple and reliable.

105

Fig 62: Typical push pull cable type system in a single screw angling boat.

REPORT EXTRACT

The free standing rudder consists of a moulded blade around a stainless steel stock. The two halves of the blade moulding are split apart where the stock emerges from the top of the blade and also running down the leading edge. Water has clearly been entering the blade for a long period and moisture levels recorded on the blade are off scale. Long term moisture ingress may have degraded the internal GRP bonding of the blade to the stock and caused corrosion in the stainless steel and welds.

Recommendation: The rudder should be unshipped and split for full inspection and repair as necessary. While it is unshipped that part of the stock normally contained in the lower bush should be carefully inspected for corrosion.

Fig 63 and 64: Typical cast aluminium steering quadrant clamped around rudder stock with a keyway.

● SECTION 11, STERN GEAR

External:

- Check prop for damage and corrosion. Most are manganese bronze and prone to dezincification. Check for pinkish pitting and gently hit the tips with a hammer. If bad small pieces will readily chip off.
- Is there any method to lock the prop nut? Is prop secure on shaft?
- Is there any play in cutless bearing? This is nearly always worst in the vertical plane.
- Is outboard bearing housing secure? Any corrosion?
- If P-bracket fitted is it secure in hull? Be brutal. Any corrosion?
- Test shaft with a magnet, if magnetic it is likely to be low grade material subject to corrosion. Some shafts are made of specialist alloys such as Aquamet which is magnetic but you are unlikely to find this in production boats. If magnetic look for brown staining immediately behind prop. If this is present ask for prop to be removed to check for crevice corrosion in taper. Rotate it by hand. Does it appear straight and free?
- If rope cutter fitted is it secure and in working order? If none suggest one be fitted for UK coastal waters due to proliferation of badly marked nets, pots etc.
- If saildrive, what is condition of leg, is it corroded or damaged?

Internal:

- Type of seal and external condition. You will need an extending mirror and powerful spotlight to examine the underside of seal. Check carefully for splits in any flexible hose commonly used to attach a stuffing box to stern tube. Failure can lead to flooding of vessel. Check also any hose clips in the installation. Stainless steel prone to corrosion on the hidden back surface in contact with the hose. If any heavy brown staining evident recommend removal for checking.
- Is seal or stuffing box secure on stern tube?
- Is stern tube secure in hull? External condition?
- Saildrive diaphragms should be replaced every seven years, any documentation? Any signs of seepage internally?

Fig 65 shows typical corrosion in a prop. Most props are made of manganese bronze which is an alloy very similar to brass and containing a good deal of zinc, thus bronze is a misnomer. In service the zinc migrates out of the metal leaving it very weak. Eventually the casting will fail. The dark pinkish pits seen here are soft enough to easily drive a spike into the prop. On the east coast this has been described for decades as the metal becoming 'carroty', which is again a reference to the colour which can sometime be quite an orange hue.

Fig 68 shows similar corrosion, this time in a feathering prop casing. This is near to perforation leading to loss of the oil within and failure of drive. Again we can see the importance of scraping away the antifouling, the simplest of investigations. This is however in line with Report Writing Fundamental Principle number two: it is only a sampling, and condition where the antifouling is untouched cannot be guaranteed.

Fig 69 shows high quality stainless steel hose clips used to secure a stuffing box to the stern tube, a very common arrangement. Both these clips fell apart when gently tapped and this would cause the boat to flood in service. This item is very often tucked away deep in the bilge and very difficult to inspect. So use an extending mirror or digital camera at arm's length. These clips are particularly prone to corrosion on the back hidden surface in contact with the hose and every check possible should always be carried out.

Fig 65: Dezincified propeller.

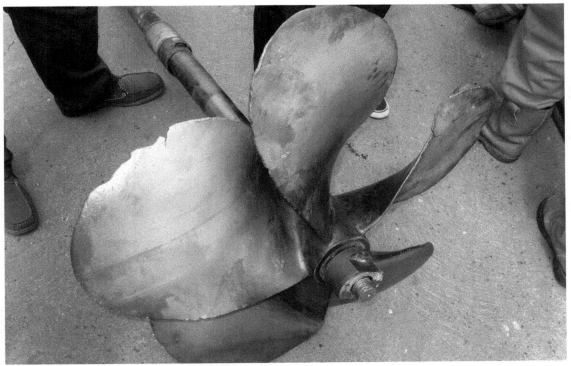

Fig 66: Tip damage and distortion, (notice tip on right). When it's this severe, prop will be out of balance causing premature wear to bushes.

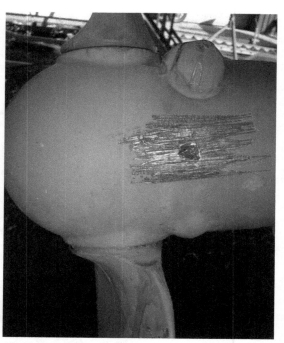

Fig 67: Corroded P-bracket. This manganese bronze P-bracket is so dezincified that is severely weakened and liable to failure. Driving in the spike resulted in a large piece just breaking away.

Fig 68: Corroded propeller casing.

Fig 69: Corroding hose clips at stern gland.

If access is really difficult they can be tapped with a very long screwdriver or crowbar resting on the screw part of the clip.

Another common area for this type of corrosion is in the clips used to secure the various bellows units in outdrive installations. The clip shown in Fig 70 was removed from such an installation and clearly shows how the corrosion occurs on the hidden back surface of the clip. Under such circumstances the clip will be damp but oxygen is excluded hard against the bellows.

Fig 70: Completely corroded stainless steel bellow clip.

These clips on outdrive legs should be regarded as a service item to be examined annually and this should be a general recommendation in all reports on these units.

You will notice a common thread in this section, the unreliability of stainless steel in the marine environment. Even the correct grades do not always perform as would reasonably be expected and every opportunity to carry out some kind of test should be taken.

It will often only be possible to examine the stern gland by extending mirror and touch, but look out for holes as in Fig 71. The hole extends right through and it is only the grease within preventing a leak.

Fig 71: Damaged and leaking hose at stern gland.

Fig 72: Deep Sea Seal.

Other types of seal seen are the Volvo boot type, which are very simple and reliable, and less commonly, seals such as the Deep Sea type in Fig 72. Also see **www.tnorrismarine.co.uk/manecraft.php** for more information.

These seals are very effective and rely upon compression in the bellows keeping two discs (one fixed, the other turning with the shaft) in constant contact, thus forming a seal. They must therefore be properly set up in accordance with the manufacturer's instructions. They can be tested by sliding the spinning disc (on the right of Fig 72) away from the fixed part to ensure there is sufficient compression in the bellows to keep the discs in good contact.

With a saildrive installation, the flexible sealing diaphragm is held into the saildrive cradle (which is GRP bonded into the hull) by a steel flange bolted in position. When seepage occurs the flange often rusts and this can be taken as an indication of seepage.

The manufacturer's recommendation is that the diaphragm is replaced every seven years so it is vital to establish if there is any history of replacement. In practice I have never known a catastrophic failure of the diaphragm (apart from when damaged) and I have frequently come across them in excess of 20 years old. However in a survey scenario it is obviously foolish not to abide by any manufacturer's recommendation.

Fig 73: Rusted flange to saildrive diaphragm.

Be particularly wary when saildrives are fitted to twin keelers because the saidrive leg has absolutely no protection from submerged objects. In extreme cases, the engine can be ripped from its mountings or even the cradle itself can de-bond.

Many people, including myself, were very sceptical about the longevity of saildrive units but in practice they have proved at least as reliable as conventional stern gear.

Bonding in a saildrive cradle must be done with the utmost care in the moulding shop because the GRP cradle itself is bought in and may have been moulded some time ago and it will thus be fully cured. Therefore the bond between it and the hull will not be a chemical bond as when the hull is moulded. The smooth moulded surface of the cradle must be properly keyed to provide a good mechanical bonding surface and in a repair situation epoxy resin would be used for its superior bonding properties.

In Fig 75, the holes for the fastenings that secure the steel diaphragm retaining flange (as illustrated in Fig 73) in position can be seen at the aft end of the cradle.

It is not unheard of for boats to be lifted with the aft sling caught on the saildrive leg so approximately half the boat's weight is being borne by the engine mounts – which suddenly find themselves under great tension – which they are not designed for, plus the bonding of the saildrive cradle.

Fig 74: Volvo Saildrive diaphragm. This is a simple single lip seal.

Fig 75: Bonding in a saildrive cradle.

I have known this happen several times and in the majority of cases absolutely no visible damage has occurred, although the engine mounts were replaced anyway. On one occasion however all was not well.

In Figs 76 to 78, the entire cradle de-bonded and the boat would have sunk had she been launched. In the event it was found that the smooth moulded cradle had not been keyed and all the bonding released cleanly just like a component being released from a mould. Had this saildrive taken an impact during normal use the boat would have sunk quickly. So always check this bonding most thoroughly and don't be afraid to use a blade as in Fig 49.

In Fig 77 we are looking at the aft end of the cradle where the diaphragm flange locates and the leg is fitted. The original GRP bonding has been pulled off the hull and cradle, lifted out and turned over to illustrate how it has just pulled off so easily and neatly as if it had been designed to!

In Figs 76 and 78 the bonding around the perimeter was no better. This is obviously scary stuff but we must not get too carried away here, a surveyor can only do what is possible without destructive testing or dismantling unless otherwise authorised to do so. He should however spot warning signs and recommend further investigation. The first time you get this right and perhaps avoid the boat having a major incident your reputation will be greatly enhanced and more work will be forthcoming.

Before we leave this section, a word on cutless bearings and similar neoprene types found on most modern yachts. It is a fact that the soft bush or bearing will often wear the hard shaft and when excess play is found in such a bearing serious wear to the shaft is frequently found when the bearing is removed. So what started as a simple cutless bearing replacement ends up with the shaft having to be built up or replaced.

Fig 76: Saildrive cradle de-bonded.

Fig 77: De-bonded saildrive cradle.

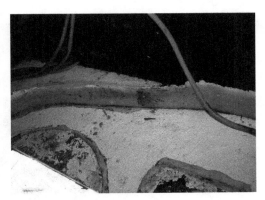
Fig 78: De-bonded saildrive cradle.

The shaft in Fig 79 has been withdrawn from its bearing and a clear ridge can be seen in the shaft on the left of the picture where the end of the bearing is normally positioned. The shaft is considerably worn in way of the bearing and will have to be built up and machined back or replaced. So remember to warn that this may be necessary when the assembly is dismantled.

Fig 79: Worn shaft in way of bearing.

Fig 80: Pitted propeller shaft.

The boat in Fig 80 has had a new shaft seal fitted leaving the old part of the shaft, previously in the stuffing box type seal, as illustrated in Fig 71, exposed. This part of the shaft would have been in contact with the gland packing and the surface has corroded. This is typical and while it is not affecting the strength of the shaft at this stage it would be very difficult to maintain a good seal as the packing would be constantly worn by the rough surface of the shaft.

REPORT EXTRACTS

Severe corrosion to poor quality prop shaft

RH two bladed manganese bronze prop on stainless steel shaft. There is some pitting to the prop but still of adequate strength. Prop nut has locking tab in position to secure. The prop was removed to reveal an extraordinary and very serious level of corrosion to the shaft mainly within the prop taper and keyway. Obviously the shaft must be replaced using an appropriate grade of austenitic stainless steel.

The shaft was tested with a magnet and found to be very magnetic, suggesting it to be of a low grade ferritic (or martensitic) stainless steel unsuitable for this application. (There are other specialised alloys such as Aquamet used in prop shafts but this is normally where a higher strength for a given diameter is required and that does not appear to be the case here.)

This type of severe rapid corrosion is sometimes associated with a current leakage from the ship but I do not think that is the case here because by chance another identical yacht was seen in the yard with the same problem and the chances of replicating a stray leakage are not high.

The corrosion would appear to have started as crevice corrosion whereby the material was deprived of oxygen but with water present within the taper. This type of corrosion will occur regardless of any cathodic protection and that is the case here, there being two shaft anodes quite close to the affected area which are part wasted. (The galvanic couple is between constituent parts of the alloy and thus is not dependent on the proximity of another dissimilar metal.) At the time of writing builder's response is that they pay for an appropriate high grade of stainless steel and that is what they expect their supplier to deliver but that is not the case here. It was also noted that the key itself, situated right in the centre of the corrosion, was of a non magnetic high grade stainless and entirely unaffected.

Shaft is supported by a bronze P-bracket, found secure in hull. Some pitting present but not serious. Excessive play was noted in the neoprene outboard bearing. This may also be due to corrosion on the shaft within the bearing but is just as likely due to the high level of silt etc in suspension in local waters. In such conditions it is my experience that this type of bearing will wear quite quickly. Note that, in this instance, having established that the prop shaft was of suspect quality, the rudder stock was tested with a magnet with the same results. Therefore a recommendation was made to drop the rudder in order that the stock could be examined inside the bush (where most wear and corrosion will normally be found) and 30% wastage was revealed. This is an obvious example of how a surveyor must follow a train of thought through from one item to another.

Subsequent analysis of the prop shaft described above confirmed it to be of poor quality and Builders replaced both the prop shaft and rudder FOC within one week.

Loose P-bracket causing leak, flexible hose at stern gland overlaminated with GRP! Possible engine misalignment.

- Shaft is supported by a bronze P-bracket bonded and bolted into hull, and the P-bracket is very loose in the hull.
- Excessive play noted in cutless bearing.

Internal:
- The GRP internal bracing for the P-bracket is minimal in this design and in this case due to damage catastrophic failure is occurring. The P-bracket is overlaminated internally forming in effect a moulded socket into which the P-bracket locates. Two bolts hold it firmly in place. In this case the entire socket is fractured in the hull and moving with the P-bracket. Access for complete inspection internally is impossible due to an additional water tank but given how easily the bracket and its socket can be moved most of the laminate must be fractured and there is also evidence of leaking through the fractures. The installation is now so weak that an impact from driftwood etc could sink the vessel.
- Stern gland and seal: This consists of a conventional stuffing box connected to the stern tube in the normal way utilising a short length of industrial hose secured with hose clips. That securing the hose to the stern tube is now entirely encapsulated in GRP as is most of the hose. The hose and retaining clips are items that need to be regularly inspected and will also need replacing during the yacht's life. In this case the GRP prevents inspection, and also begs the question as to why it was put there in the first place. Access was restricted but the stern tube itself is secure in the hull where seen.
- As described below in section 29 the forward engine mounting plates have disintegrated. Given this and the condition of the cutless bearing, P-bracket and the GRP which has been applied around the stern tube, it is considered very likely that severe misalignment of the engine is present, or has been at some time in the past.

Recommendations:
- The engine alignment should be checked. (No work to the P-bracket should be commenced until engine alignment and position of P-bracket are confirmed as correct.)
- The excess GRP laminations at the stern tube covering the flexible link and its retaining clip should be removed and the link and clip checked.
- The P-bracket attachment is in hazardous condition and liable to catastrophic failure. It will be necessary to rebuild the 'socket' into which the bracket locates and it would also be advisable to introduce additional reinforcing, this consisting of athwartships GRP knees formed over 20mm plywood. The knees should be the full height of the bracket and tapered off to nothing over about 150mm.
- The cutless bearing should be replaced.

Split hose at stern gland

- Stern gland and seal: This consists of a stuffing box connected to stern tube via a short length of industrial hose. Access to this is extremely awkward but it does appear that the hose is split, with one of the aftermost hose clips possibly cutting into it.
- Stern tube seen secure in hull.

Recommendation:
The short length of industrial hose connecting the stuffing box to the stern tube should be replaced.

● SECTION 12, CATHODIC PROTECTION

- A good working knowledge of the galvanic series is essential. **www.corrosionsource.com/ handbook/galv_series.htm** is an excellent resource for further technical information.
- Look for any obvious galvanic action. If present, investigate why, although a full analysis is outside the scope of a routine survey and will require a specialist. Take a good deal of time. When very rapid corrosion has taken place i.e. months not years, suspect current leakage not galvanic action. With the proliferation of shore power supplies this has become a very complex area where even experts cannot always agree. Galvanic isolators are now inexpensive and will often solve unidentified problems.
- Hammer sound any anode studs (without damaging the threads). If the anodes become fully wasted the studs can take over the sacrificial role and corrode away.
- Check continuity from anode to stern gear with circuit tester. Many surveyors today feel that skin fittings do not require bonding to anodes unless special circumstances apply.
- If shaft anode fitted is it secure?
- Do anodes require replacement and are they not antifouled over?

One of the acknowledged leaders in this field is MG Duff and their website **www.mgduff.co.uk** contains a wealth of information including downloads.

Fig 81 was taken inside a GRP yacht where the anode had been allowed to waste away completely and in effect the steel mounting studs, being the least noble metal in this particular system, took over the anode's role with somewhat alarming consequences. The studs were rusting severely and one fell out of the boat when tapped from outside. This is quite extreme and there may have been some element of current leakage involved but again the emphasis here is finding the defect in the first place, that is paramount. Such defects will often not be found by a visual inspection only, some kind of additional physical test such as a simple tap is required.

Fig 81: Corroding anode stud.

● SECTION 13, SKIN FITTINGS AND OTHER THROUGH HULL APERTURES

It is suggested a form of wording as below be included in survey reports and that this forms the basis of the examination:

No skin fittings or valves were dismantled as part of this survey but the following routine tests were carried out:

- Examination from outside and inside the boat.
- All valves opened and closed to their full extent.
- Any fixing bolts hammer tested where accessible.
- Bodies of the valves or seacocks tested with a hammer inside the boat and external parts hammer tested outside the boat.
- Fittings aggressively tested inside the boat for security in the hull.
- Hose clips inspected and hoses aggressively tested for security.

- Is there clear access to all fittings from inside the boat? If not, mention this and recommend improving access. It's often a case of out of sight out of mind.
- Check condition of all fittings inside and outside boat. Aggressively test for security in hull (but not between tides).
- Record type of valve etc and function for all through hull fittings. Obviously tie up the fittings visible externally with those internally. It's a good idea to record where the access to each fitting is inside the boat in the survey report, this may be much appreciated.
- Check external condition of all valves and operate them in both directions to the full extent of their travel. If these are gatevalves apply considerable torque to the handle, if the stem breaks it was defective anyway.
- Are all hoses secure and clips in good condition? It is best practice to fit double clips but tailpipes often not long enough. Sometimes two clips in this situation can encourage the hose to actually come off. Remember too that clips can occasionally cut into hoses. In particular check the clips on the INBOARD end of cockpit drains. These are usually very inaccessible up under the cockpit sole but are most important because everybody leaves cockpit drain valves open, so if the hose becomes detached and drops the boat will flood.
- Beware plain nylon fittings close to waterline where loosely stowed heavy items inside the boat can sheer the fitting off in heavy weather, particularly when very cold. They also become brittle with age. Always give this warning where applicable. They are also subject to UV degrading externally and may crack just inside the fitting, with the flange eventually sheering off. Such fittings must never be used below the waterline. Never accept plastic seacocks even of approved type in engine spaces. Even a small fire will render them useless. (This is a stipulation of the MCA Code.)
- Don't forget transducers, grounding plates, skin fittings for some refrigeration units, in fact all through hull fittings must be checked and recorded. Plastic log impellor housings relying on an external flange and plastic nut internally should be lightly overlaminated inside the boat so the unit will remain in situ if the flange sheers off, which is rare but has happened.

Before we look at defects in this section it is necessary to describe the components involved. There are three different types of valve in common use below the waterline and it is necessary to get the terminology right and understand how each works.

Fig 82 shows the most common type now in almost universal use in new production boats; the ballvalve. This valve is threaded onto a separate bronze through hull fitting and has a rotating chromium plated ball seating on neoprene seals. The valves are made of Dezincification Resistant Brass (DZR) to specification DZR1 (BSEN 1982 CC752C). This is a special alloy for die casting and approved for use in the marine environment.

The gatevalve is exactly what it says, a gate, rather like in a lock gate, screws up and down to open and close the aperture. Both ballvalves and gatevalves will be threaded onto bronze through hull fittings which are a separate component.

Fig 84 shows the king of them all, the seacock. This is still made by Blakes of Gosport, **www.blakes-lavac-taylors.co.uk/index.htm**. These components are bolted (and sometimes also FRP laminated) into the boat and have a tapered hollow plug locating in a tapered body. When the gallery in the taper lines up with the inlet in the body the seacock is open. For decades these have been made of bronze but in the last few years production has also switched to the DZR1 (BSEN 1982 CC752C) specification like ballvalves. The supplied fixing bolts are of phosphor bronze.

Fig 82: Standard ballvalve. Note most have mild steel coated handles which rust as is happening here.

Fig 83: Standard gatevalve.

Fig 84: Standard bronze seacock.

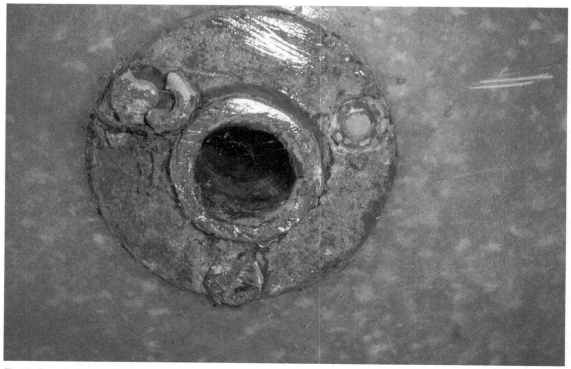

Fig 85: Corroded seacock bolts.

Fig 86: Corroded copper tail pipe on seacock.

It is not unusual to encounter seacocks 50 years old and still in good working order. There are also reinforced plastic versions of the seacock but these are quite unusual. The best known are manufactured by Forespar in the USA, **www.forespar.com** and these are made to ABYC approved standards.

Through hull fittings made of unreinforced plastics such as nylon and Delrin are widely used above the waterline.

Fig 85 shows the results of using bolts made from the wrong material to secure a heads discharge skin fitting into the hull. The bolts are almost certainly brass and have dezincified leaving the weakened metal a pinkish hue as already seen on the propeller and P-bracket illustrated in section 11. Again the point to note here is that all the nuts 'appeared' intact and sound like the one in the bottom of the picture which was not tested. The others were tested by tapping with a screwdriver and hammer with the most satisfying results, one bolt sheered and both nuts disintegrated. If I still have to make a case for applying tests then this is a good one.

Never lose sight of the fact that failure of any skin fitting may sink the vessel.

Bolts securing bronze seacocks should always be of the same alloy, (or very similar) as the unit itself and supplied by the manufacturer of the seacock.

Stainless steel is often used in this application where replacements become necessary and given its unreliable performance in this kind of application and already seen in section 10 it is always wise to suggest drawing of a bolt for full inspection at time of survey and annually thereafter.

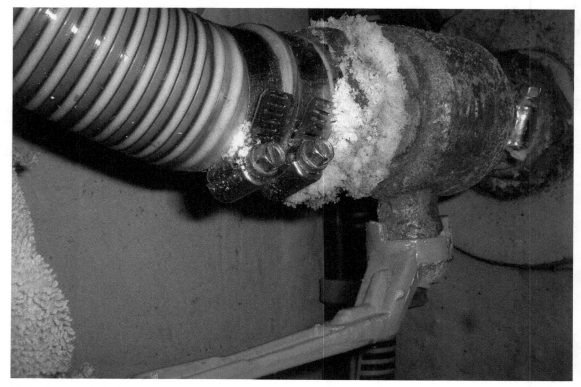

Fig 87: Corroding ballvalve.

Copper tail pipes are quite often found on skin fittings and in my experience its performance is variable in this application. Copper is a comparatively noble metal and copper fastenings in wooden boats frequently last 100 years. However in this application the thin walled tubing will often corrode in a few years as was the case in Fig 86.

There are enough indications in Fig 87 to recommend dismantling of this ballvalve for full inspection. There is clearly some unusual activity here probably associated with current leakage. Look too at the securing hose clips which are showing brown staining around the threads.

Fig 88 shows another compelling case for carrying out simple tests. This gatevalve 'appeared' sound but once tested with a screwdriver gently tapped with a hammer the body was found to be badly corroded and disintegrated. The valve operated normally prior to the test.

The problem with gatevalves is that they vary enormously in quality, and once one has been in place for a few years a surveyor is not going to be able to positively identify it. They are made in their millions in ordinary brass and many of these end up in boats, as is obviously the case in Fig 88. So it is of the utmost importance to test these items and record the details in the report.

In most instances (and with careful preparation) it is a straightforward job to unscrew the gatevalve from the through hull fitting (which can then be thoroughly inspected) and fit a new DZR ballvalve in its place. Given the availability of relatively inexpensive ballvalves of known quality it is good practice to simply

Fig 88: Gatevalve ready to sink the boat.

replace old gatevalves given their unpredictability. Beware of through hull fittings and tailpipes, or any other component in the assembly, made of TONVAL.

This is basically brass and totally unsuitable for use below the waterline due to its tendency to dezincify and disintegrate just like the gatevalve in Fig 89. Don't overlook log fittings and echo sounder transducers. Fig 92 shows an old log fitting is bolted in place and again under test the bolts disintegrated. This fitting is ready to fall out of the boat.

Fig 90 shows a more modern paddle wheel log fitting in a plastic housing, and this kind of fitting is in almost universal use. The plastic is unreinforced and the external flange can sheer off allowing the unit to come loose into the boat leaving a 1.5" hole. This example is even worse because the fitting has been installed where only part of the flange is in contact with the hull, and the resulting gap has merely been made good with soft filler. This has placed an unfair strain on the fitting from day one. Such fittings must always be installed where both the outer flange and inner nut are lying tight and square to the hull surface. Another related point to remember is that plywood or hardwood pads are often fitted inside behind the securing nut. If that is the case the timber must be sealed with epoxy to prevent water penetration and consequent swelling of the timber, which will place additional strain on a fitting perhaps already over tightened when installed.

Even when properly installed the flanges will occasionally sheer.

Fig 89: Corroded bolts in log housing.

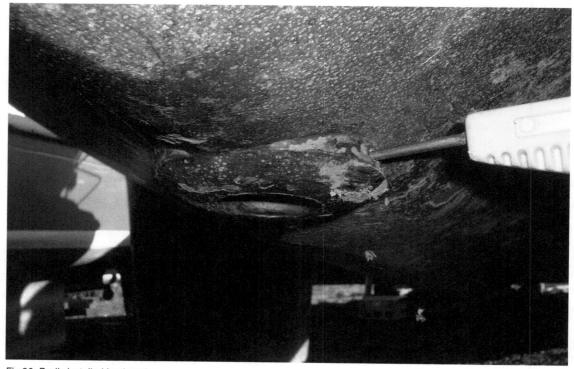

Fig 90: Badly installed log housing.

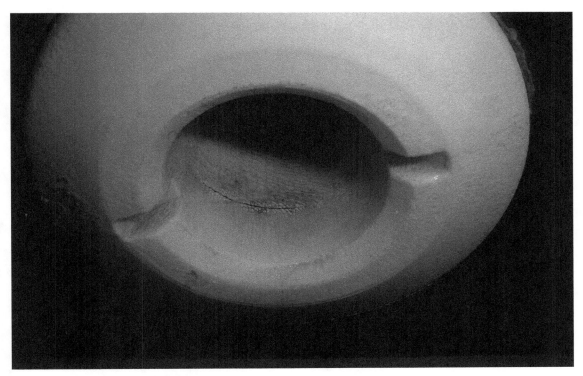

Fig 91: Cracked plastic through hull fitting.

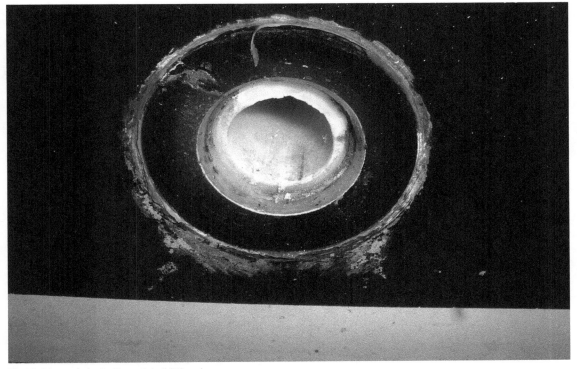

Fig 92: Sheared plastic through hull fitting.

Staying with plastic fittings, Fig 91 shows a typical unreinforced nylon or similar through hull skin fitting, there are literally millions in use. They are specifically not for use below the waterline but are quite often found in that application. More commonly they are found just above the waterline as in this case. The fitting here is clearly cracked and weakened, and it is only a few inches above the waterline so if the fitting fails any slight rolling of the vessel, for example when left on the mooring, will result in ingress and rapid flooding once the hole is immersed.

These fittings are often encountered inside lockers with anchors and other heavy gear loosely stowed nearby and any motion puts the fitting in danger of being sheered off, particularly in very cold weather when the material is brittle. On many modern motor yachts these are often found close to the waterline and sealed behind fixed linings.

Fig 91 shows a typical plastic through hull fitting. Not only is the fitting cracked, but the material is badly UV degraded as can be seen by the hundreds of tiny cracks visible in the surface.

Fig 92 shows the same fitting after just a gentle tap. It can now clearly be seen that only about one third of the flange was still sound (that part of the plastic that appears clean), the rest has been cracked for a long period allowing water etc to discolour it. Note that the length of the perimeter which is clearly defective is much longer than the length of the visible crack in Fig 91.

A recurring theme in this book is the essential requirement for practical tests and this is another example. These fittings are frequently found with no visible cracks but sheer off when tested and in Fig 92 it can be seen just how close to the waterline this fitting was. Of course the recommendation would be to replace it with bronze.

Don't forget the hoses and pipework. The wall of the hose in Fig 93 is paper thin where it has been in contact with something hot, probably the engine exhaust. This was not visible from the obvious viewpoints and emphasises the requirement to access all possible areas, even if this is awkward and time consuming.

This part of the hose is below the waterline and being a cockpit drain the valve is always left open...

This section is where the majority of serious but easily remedied defects are found, and sinkings as a result of failure in this vital area are commonplace.

No survey extracts are included here, it is just down to proper inspection and common sense.

For those wishing to produce a survey report, some standard wording is included in the last chapter on report writing.

Fig 93: Damaged cockpit drain hose.

CHAPTER 8: **INSPECTION SECTIONS 14-20**

The next sub heading from the survey report covers sections 14–20.

⬤ ON DECK

14. **Main companionway and other accesses to accommodation**
15. **Ports, windows etc**
16. **Pulpit, stanchions, pushpit, lifelines and jackstays**
17. **Rigging attachment points**
18. **Ground tackle and mooring arrangements**
19. **Other deck gear and fittings**
20. **Davits and boarding ladders**

Some of the sections in this chapter are common sense and require little explanation, comment or illustration by report extracts.

⬤ SECTION 14, MAIN COMPANIONWAY AND OTHER ACCESS TO ACCOMMODATION

- Security and condition of main hatch. Plywood hatchboards sound? If the vessel is an offshore type are all hatches properly watertight and in a position so as not to allow premature downflooding?
- For offshore can the hatch be operated and secured from deck and below? Can hatch boards be secured in place independently of the sliding hatch? Many forehatches are now hinged on their aft edge (often due to the position of a babystay) and this is generally considered acceptable.
- Condition and type of all other hatches. Any perspex crazing? Hatches generally sound? If a hatch is clearly an escape route from that part of the vessel, is it actually large enough for this purpose?
- Hinges intact and secure method of closure provided?
- Gaskets intact, any signs of seepage from below?

⬤ SECTION 15, PORTS, WINDOWS ETC

- Are the ports lying tight and fair to the coamings externally?
- Thousands of production boats have been built with aluminium framed ports fixed with stainless steel bolts and chrome plated brass dome nuts known as internuts. In use the aluminium frames and the internuts corrode.
- Random test any fastenings with a screwdriver.
- Many ports are now simply bonded in position and when the hull flexes these can become loose. So give them a tap with your clenched fist in the direction away from the bonding.
- If set in rubber of limited strength not suitable for offshore.
- Crazing to perspex? If surface mounted look for splits around the fastenings.
- If glass is it toughened?
- General condition plus gaskets if of opening type.
- Leaks from below?

REPORT EXTRACTS

Corroding window frames

All the ports are of aluminium framed toughened glass and some corrosion is present in the frames. This type of port utilises aluminium frames with stainless steel bolts and chromed brass dome nuts, (known as internuts), thus some corrosion is inevitable. Fastenings were sampled at random in the eight ports and were found to be holding well. The ports are currently considered satisfactory but some failure of fastenings and further corrosion to the frames over the next year or two is inevitable.

Crazed perspex windows

Vessel fitted with eight aluminium framed fixed perspex ports. Some crazing present and the worst crazed windows should be replaced for serious offshore use.

Some corrosion is present in the aluminium frames. This type of port utilises aluminium frames with stainless steel and chrome plated brass fastenings, thus corrosion is inevitable, but still considered secure and serviceable.

Failure of bonding

The polycarbonate lights are bonded in place and when gentle pressure was applied to that by the chart table it simply fell out.

Recommendation: Given the failure of the port close to the chart table all other ports that are bonded in place should be checked.

● SECTION 16, PULPIT, STANCHIONS, PUSHPIT, LIFELINES AND JACKSTAYS

- Security and general condition. Aluminium bases very prone to vertical splitting due to build up of oxide in the socket. If any item has been wrenched check very carefully for any consequent damage to the deck and structure. Stanchions become very powerful levers when weight is applied. Where stanchions are attached to an aluminium toerail any wrenching could make the hull deck joint (bolted via the toerail bolts) leak. Wherever possible check the underside of fixings for seepage, corrosion and sufficient backing pads, reinforcing in the laminate etc.
- Always check plastic covered wire lifelines with a magnet. If magnetic they are galvanised wire and prone to rust unseen under the sheathing. Condemn them. Talurit type terminals are frequently found on lifelines and if the wire is stainless they must be of copper, or if galvanised wire they must be of aluminium, but occasionally one finds these mixed up, if so should be condemned.
- Security of all lashings, are they UV degraded?
- Are all jackstays and attachment points secure? Terylene webbing is very prone to UV degrading and chafe to the stitching where the eyes are formed each end. Carefully check this, someone's life may depend on it. Are any shackles locked up with seizing wire or cable ties?

Fig 94: Wrenched pushpit foot.

Fig 95: Broken strands of guardrail wire.

Fig 94 shows a typical wrenched pushpit foot and while the pushpit was still secure enough it didn't end there. A long term leak via the fixing bolts had spread along the laminate, rotting the plywood backing pad incorporated into the moulding. The pad was a long piece of ply serving both the pushpit and aft mooring cleat which was severely weakened, with the bolts about to pull through the soft plywood. All this was only found because the plywood lining panel under the deckhead was damp and slightly stained and was thus removed.

● SECTION 17, RIGGING ATTACHMENT POINTS

This is one of the most important areas in a sailing vessel and one where numerous defects are found.

- Check for any obvious movement, distorting to deck, stress cracks in fitting etc. Where U-bolts are used it is important that the bolts are following the line of the rigging attached to them in a nice fair line otherwise excess stress is placed on the fitting. One often sees vertical U-bolts with lower shrouds attached at an unfair angle.
- Access is often very restricted or impossible from inside the boat. Where this is the case use a moisture meter on linings etc looking for seepage. If this has been present long term, crevice corrosion may be present in the hidden stainless steel components. Recommend dismantling for full inspection.
- Test on deck with a long crowbar using a hardwood block as a pivot placed on a plywood pad to avoid damage to deck. Get as much leverage as possible and be brutal.
- Are fittings lying tight and fair to deck? If seepage is present and they are bolted to bulkheads these may be rotten particularly behind GRP bonding. Hammer sound and spike test.
- When heavy brown staining to the fixing nuts etc is present crevice corrosion is probably developing in the threads. The shanks of U-bolts are also very vulnerable where they pass through the deck. Tap all accessible internal nuts and bolts with a hammer and screwdriver.
- Where arrangements are in place to dissipate the stresses into other parts of the structure, i.e. tie rods or plates attached to knees etc bonded into the topsides check the topsides and adjacent structure externally for distortion. It is essential to state in all reports in this section whether the rig was set up hard or not (or obviously if mast unstepped). If the rigging is slack defects may become apparent when it is set up.
- Is the forestay fitting merely bolted to the deck or does it have a plate running down the stem or similar to transfer some of the loadings into the hull? Check all welds for stress cracks.
- If the rigging has been slacked off prior to survey ask yourself why and aggressively swig the shrouds etc.

Fig 96 shows a typical stress crack along a weld in a stemhead fitting to which the forestay attaches. The crack is travelling aft along the weld and the tang is severely weakened. This type of vertical tang welded to a base plate typically has two or three holes where the forestay attaches and the forward most hole is in use as

Fig 96: Crack in weld.

Fig 97: Corroding stainless steel bolt.

was the case here. This forwardmost position is often forward of all the bolt fixings thus placing an unfair strain on the plate. So always check the position of the forestay attachment in use in relation to the bolt fastenings.

Fig 97 shows a stainless bolt removed from a conventional stainless steel chain plate bolted through the topsides of a bluewater yacht. The bolt is severely corroded immediately under the head and with the pitting established in the shank future corrosion would be quite rapid. Whatever claims are made for this material, and in spite of assurances from metallurgists, my experience has been that even the highest grades found in production boatbuilding are very unpredictable in the marine environment.

I am firmly convinced that the shanks of bolts like this sometimes pick up tiny scratches when they are first driven through their holes and this microscopic damage to the surface sustained when the boat was built creates the perfect conditions for crevice corrosion to start if moisture is introduced when seepage occurs. This is also true for rigging U-bolts where perhaps the pair of holes drilled through the deck do not quite line up with the shanks.

In fact it is a good idea to get this image fixed in your mind when inspecting parts of the vessel where stainless steel bolts are used.

Fig 98 shows the nut removed from the bolt in Fig 97. None of the corrosion evident on the back surface which could not be seen with the nut in position.

Another defect occasionally seen in nuts securing U-bolts is stress cracks in the wall. There are no other outward signs of deterioration in this nut (Fig 99) but the wall is cracked right through. Sometimes tapping the nuts inside the boat will cause them to disintegrate.

Fig 100 shows quite a common arrangement with a steel knee under the forestay fitting GRP bonded into the stem. Being in the anchor well this area is subject to damp with consequent corrosion. In Fig 100 it is obvious but less so is the fact that the stainless steel bolts pass through a plywood pad which will retain moisture and promote corrosion in the bolts when long term seepage occurs as has been the case here. Water will also run down the knee ending up at its base, causing heavy rusting and failure where it is bonded into the stem. A crowbar inserted behind the knee and used gently caused the base to pull out from the FRP bonding where it had disintegrated. Its function as a knee to transfer loadings away from the deck had long since ceased. Another worthwhile test.

Fig 98: Corroding stainless steel nut.

Fig 101 shows a stainless steel nut on a rigging U-bolt where seepage has occurred over a long period. This is an extreme example of what can happen to stainless steel in this application but to get this picture it was necessary to remove linings inside the boat which had just returned from a 15 year circumnavigation. This is one of the U-bolts on the mizzen rigging of a ketch so it would be subject to severe loadings when the mizzen was used in heavy weather.

Although no ready access was possible inside the boat, applying the block and crowbar test to the U-bolt on deck immediately produced movement and water oozing out from under the deck plate, another example championing the value of a simple little test.

Fig 99: Split stainless steel nut.

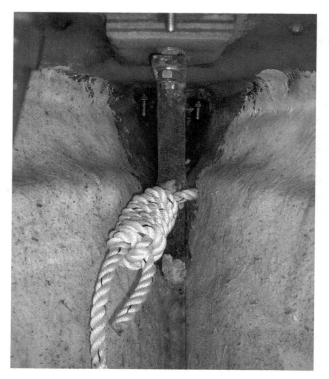

The nut is disintegrating and when the U-bolt was removed the shanks were found to be severely corroded. There has obviously been long term seepage here so it is essential to check that all deck plates etc which have a sealing function on deck are lying tight and fair to the deck. A feeler gauge is useful in this respect for pushing under fittings to find any gap, however small, where water might enter.

Obviously load bearing fittings such as this are always going to be subject to movement and seepage. Obviously when one component in a series of similar ones is found to be defective the recommendation is to dismantle them all for checking.

Fig 102 is an obvious example of a lifting chain plate but there is another sign here which should be recognised and

Fig 100: Corroding knee under forestay fitting.

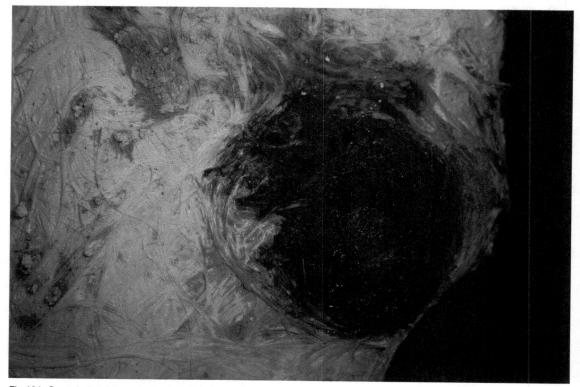

Fig 101: Corroded stainless steel nut on U-bolt.

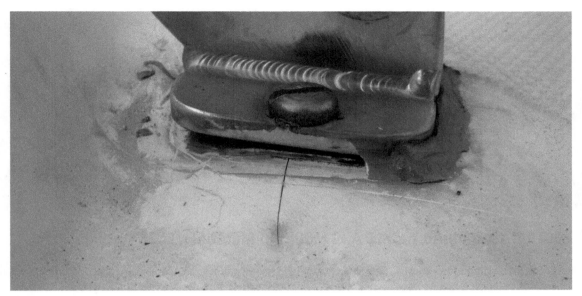

Fig 102: Lifting chain plate.

appreciated. This is a load bearing fitting holding the rig up and the previous remedy for this serious problem has been to apply some filler around the plate. If this cavalier attitude to maintenance has been applied throughout the boat then the prudent surveyor or potential purchaser will be on high alert.

REPORT EXTRACTS

Severe crevice corrosion to rigging U-bolts shanks

All the other attachment points for both the main and mizzen masts consist of stainless steel U-bolts fitted through the deck or coachroof. Access was only possible to the following:

Mizzen port cap and aft lower shroud U-bolts accessible in port cockpit locker behind a wiring conduit. These are both partially GRP encapsulated and much staining and corrosion is evident (Fig 101). The photo shows the underside of one of the two nuts on the U-bolt and a good deal of corrosion is clearly present to the stainless steel. Under such conditions where oxygen is excluded but moisture is present due to seepage this type of corrosion is quite common, the threads inside the nuts and the shanks of the U-bolts where they pass through the deck being particularly vulnerable. The corresponding U-bolts on the stb side are entirely GRP encapsulated and no access was possible but aggressive non destructive testing on deck produced movement and evidence of seepage.

Recommendation: As described in the text good access inside the boat was only possible to three of the fourteen identical rigging attachment U-bolts. Having identified serious corrosion to one of these the remainder should be fully inspected. This will involve a good deal of dismantling to linings etc. (Subsequent dismantling revealed shanks of U-bolts near to failure.)

Severe crevice corrosion to rigging U-bolts fixing nuts.

Extensive brown staining is present to the underside of all the rigging U-bolts, backing plates and fixing nuts. When the nuts on the port capshroud U-bolt were gently tapped they broke into pieces.

Recommendation: All the rigging U-bolts should be removed for full inspection and replacement as required.

● SECTION 18, GROUND TACKLE AND MOORING ARRANGEMENTS

- When inspecting areas such as this, do bear in mind that what may be elementary and obvious to you will not be so to a novice boat owner, or indeed a novice in charge of an experienced owner's vessel. If an accident occurs you may find yourself being held liable if you have not identified obvious hazards etc.
- Adequate for vessel? If you do not lay out any chains for inspection link by link then record this limitation in the report. Check wear to any moving parts on anchors. Are any shackles used securely locked (moused) up to prevent the pins unwinding?
- For coastal and offshore the MCA harmonised code is useful for reference. If in the general preparation with the client you have established what kind of use he proposes for the vessel establish whether the ground tackle is adequate for that proposed use.
- Cleats, bollards etc secure? Adequate reinforcing in the laminate, backing pads etc? If of plywood beware of rot if the fixing bolts have been leaking.
- Provision to prevent chain jumping in heavy weather?
- Any winches secure and in working order? Electrics associated with any winch often located in damp anchor locker, any signs of corrosion?
- Common sense and observation should be sufficient here. Include more detail if client requires so, i.e. you have established a specific use for the vessel and have been asked to assess the vessel accordingly.

● SECTION 19, OTHER DECK GEAR AND FITTINGS

- A common sense general appraisal is sufficient, the main criteria being security of all fittings and, for those with moving parts, mechanical wear.
- If highly stressed look for wear and fatigue cracks to stainless steel and aluminium components (particularly racing and blue water boats).

● SECTION 20, DAVITS AND BOARDING LADDERS

- General condition and security. Working order?
- Does any folding ladder extend well below waterline to aid recovery of man overboard?
- Is the structure to which the above are attached strong enough? Look for stress cracks or fractures around davit feet, and adequate backing pads underneath.

CHAPTER 9: **INSPECTION SECTIONS 21-24**

The next sub heading from the survey report covers sections 21–24

● **RIG**

21. **Spars**
22. **Standing rigging**
23. **Running rigging**
24. **Sails and covers etc**

● **SECTION 21, SPARS**

- Please, if the mast is stepped do not make ridiculous statements like, 'the mast and rigging was examined by binocular and all 'appeared' satisfactory'. This kind of test cannot detect stress cracks etc and conveys a totally false sense of security to the client.
- Any damage or distortion to the basic extrusions? Many masts are joined from new, is the joint lying tight and associated rivets plus the extrusion around them free from corrosion? Is the mast standing in column and undistorted?

Fig 104: Crack in mast wall.

- If keel stepped expect corrosion at the mast heel and under the boot where mast passes through deck.
- Are all fittings that are accessible secure and free from stress cracks, particularly rigging attachment points? Pay particular attention to the type of spreader socket consisting of a stainless steel tube welded to a base plate, this riveted to mast. Look for fatigue cracks in the welds.
- Is there undue corrosion to rivets and other fastenings or more commonly the aluminium around them? With the inevitable mixing of metals corrosion is inevitable. If there is corrosion around the perimeter of a stainless steel fitting it will inevitably be worse underneath the fitting. Any perforation under fittings amounts to a substantial loss of strength in the extrusion wall and must be condemned.
- Is the anodising faded, damaged or breached?
- Are any winches etc in working order?
- If mast stepped, aggressively swig the main shrouds to check for any movement where the spreader sockets are attached to the mast.

Fig 104 shows a crack in the mast wall, and the previous repair was to fill it with epoxy! The crack had travelled between holes in the extrusion where a fitting had been removed. Again this is indicative of past maintenance quality and alarm bells will be ringing.

Fig 105: Spreaders correctly set.

Figs 106 and 107: Stress cracks in spreader sockets.

In Fig 105 we see how with standard masthead rigs, spreaders should dissect the angle where they meet the cap shrouds and be prevented from moving when the leeward cap shroud is not under full tension.

Figs 106 and 107 show typical stress cracking around the base of a spreader socket. When this is severe it can sometimes be detected by swigging the shrouds from deck level at which time movement will be visible between the socket and base plate. Occasionally they will sheer off under this test, providing great job satisfaction. Fig 107 also has sheared rivets and is not far from losing the mast.

Fig 108: Heavy corrosion in way of stainless steel spreader fitting.

Fig 109: Severe corrosion to mast heel.

Fig 110: Typical corrosion where stainless steel and aluminium are used.

With the level of corrosion around the perimeter, as seen in Fig 108, it is almost inevitable that it will be worse under the fitting. Fig 109 shows typical corrosion found at the mast heel with keel stepped masts. Both the heel casting and extrusion wall are corroding but a simple repair can be made by cutting the extrusion back to sound metal then bonding the heel casting back with epoxy glue (thus avoiding the mixing of metals, which has caused the problem due to their distance apart in the galvanic series). A hardwood pad or similar is then inserted under the mast step to make up the lost height.

Fig 110 shows corrosion around a stainless steel fastening at a mast heel but this kind of corrosion will occur in the marine environment anywhere the two metals are used. Modern masts make great use of welded aluminium fittings and every effort is made to avoid the mixing of metals.

REPORT EXTRACT

Loose spreader sockets and general appraisal of mast.

Examined unstepped on trestles. The silver anodised Z spars mast found in good condition with no distortion or damage. The anodising is not unduly worn or faded.

There is no serious corrosion around fittings and rivets. All fittings were found secure apart from the spreader brackets which are loose where they are riveted to the mast, particularly that on the stb side. Both are in hazardous condition.

A stainless steel crane carries the backstay at the mast head and this is constructed with stainless steel bolts or studding used as spacers between the two cheeks of the crane. However it was noted that some of the washers used are of mild steel and these are rusting badly. When they start to disintegrate the bolts will be rendered loose and this may lead to failure of the crane.

Recommendation: Both spreader brackets require re-fastening to the mast. The rusting mild steel washers used on the backstay crane at the masthead should be replaced with new of A4 grade stainless steel. All bolts and studding used in the construction must be secure with locking nuts or the ends of the studding peened over to secure the nuts.

● SECTION 22, STANDING RIGGING

- Try to establish age. If broker's or vendor's spec claims it has been renewed is the invoice for the work available? Any claims for work done must be verified.
- Any visible damage to wire? If roller reefing fitted check particularly where the forestay emerges from the top of luffspar (if mast unstepped).
- Examine all stainless steel terminals, rigging screws, toggles etc for stress cracks.
- Are adequate toggles fitted to allow good articulation of rigging? If fork to fork rigging screws are used the top and bottom forks should be set at right angles to each other, thus offering maximum articulation.
- Are all split pins etc intact? If any shackles are used, are they locked with seizing wire?
- Examine all components for stress cracks under x10 magnification.
- Highly recommend resistance testing of terminals, i.e. Maidsure Rigtester. In the absence of this if the mast is unstepped bend the wire to about 45 degrees where it leaves the terminals. If the wire is

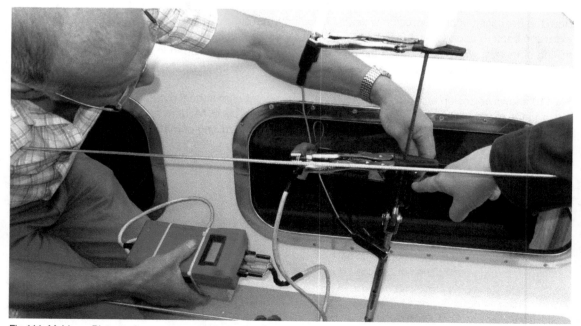

*Fig 111: Maidsure Rigtester in use. **www.maidsure.org.uk***

fatigued this may produce broken strands.

- If mast is stepped and has t-bar type upper terminals, are these lying in a straight fair line with the rigging wire? Commonly the terminals do not fit properly in the keyholes and prevent this. When the wire is not lying straight and fair to the terminal, fatigue will occur in the wire after multiple slack/tension cycles, i.e. when rolling for a long period. Always remove these terminals from the mast to check the bearing surfaces for stress cracks.
- If copper talurit type terminals, check for any movement of the wire within the terminal. Both parts of the wire must be lying in the terminal parallel to each other. If the end of the wire has pulled into the

Fig 112: Defective rigging terminal!

terminal it may fail. Check also for broken strands in the tight turn of the wire round the thimble.

The terminal in Fig 112 appeared intact but was found to have such a high resistance when electronically tested that it was off scale and the meter would not read. The outer strands of wire were then teased out from the neck of the terminal with a spike and as can be seen a number were sheered. Worse was the state of the inner core where the majority of strands were sheered and had been that way for some time. Many surveyors condemn the use of electronic testing but that is because they do not understand its use or limitations, or they won't invest in the equipment. While this kit is not perfect it is better than doing nothing and the above is a compelling argument for its use. While this may have been revealed with a simple bend test, with mast unstepped it could not be seen with the rigging in tension.

Beware a type of old fashioned stainless steel terminal which has no taper visible in the neck, this creates a hard spot where the flexible wire enters the rigid terminal body and accelerates fatigue. These are seldom seen now and should be condemned.

Always inspect the forestay very carefully where it emerges from the top of the reefing gear luffspar. This area is vulnerable to damage and with some types if the gear jams the wire can be unlayed as in Fig 113. Obviously once this has happened the wire must be condemned even if it is much less severe than shown here.

In Fig 114 the flexible wire does not leave the rigid terminal bodies in a good fair line. Every time this wire goes through a slack/tension cycle, i.e. when the boat is rolling heavily, the wire moves at the neck of the terminal, promoting premature fatigue. This is a graphic example of how important good articulation is in standing rigging systems and that must be borne in mind throughout the rig inspection.

Always be thinking of the stresses the wire and components will be subject to when the vessel is underway in differing conditions. The first thing to try here is to slack the rigging off and attempt to re-align the top terminals in their keyholes, but if this is not successful the rigging will have to be replaced. This situation is quite commonly seen when new rigging has been made up using terminals not suited to the particular mast.

Copper compression terminals as in Figs 116 and 117 are only used on 1x19 wire up to 6mm because of the very tight turn required in the wire to render round the thimble, although they can be used in very large sizes with wires of different construction, i.e. a large number of smaller, more flexible individual strands. If this type of terminal is used it is essential that the two strands of wire are lying straight and parallel to each other when the terminal is applied. If they are not, the terminal becomes tapered when it is compressed and is liable to failure.

Fig 113: Defective forestay.

Fig 114: Defective alignment of upper rigging terminals.

Fig 115: This shows a T-bar type terminal removed from the mast. These terminals have been much improved but some examples will still be found where cracks occur on the bearing surface and they should always be removed from their slots for full inspection. This example has a piece actually chipped out of it.

Fig 116: This terminal has one obvious broken strand but there are also two more at the top right of the copper terminal.

Fig 117: This terminal is sound but would lay your hand open if you grabbed it at sea.

A situation is sometimes encountered with headsail reefing gears where the hole in the original stemhead fitting dictates the diameter of the forestay clevis pin but the holes in the two reefing gear fixing cheeks are much larger. When that is the case it may be possible for the clevis pin to pull through, taking its split pin or locking ring with it. To prevent this, well-fitting washers should be fitted on the clevis pin.

Never underestimate the potential of vibration and resonance, the effects of which have to be seen to be believed. This is particularly the case where a vessel has been ashore for a long period on concrete hard standing with the mast stepped, in fact under such circumstances it is good practice to recommend unstepping of the mast for full inspection.

So far we have looked at stainless steel swaged terminals and copper compression type. Stainless steel swages are by far the most common and in universal use on new production boats. They have improved over the years and the vertical cracks often seen in the necks are now rare. The use of copper compression type on production boats is now restricted to backstay bridles which are required to render around a sheave and 7x7 wire is used in lieu of 1x19.

The last type of terminal commonly seen is the mechanical type known as Sta-lok and Norseman, **www. stalok.com** and **www.lewmar.com**. See Fig 119.

Both use the same principle of inserting a cone into the wire which is compressed into a terminal body by simply threading the two parts together. This type is the most reliable in my experience and much liked by blue water sailors because rigging can be made up onboard and the terminals can be dismantled for inspection.

Fig 118: All clevis pins must be of the correct diameter and with secure locking arrangements.

Fig 119: Mechanical rigging terminal.

Fig 120: 1x19 stainless steel wire.

Standing rigging on production boats is nearly always of 1x19 stainless steel wire, i.e. 19 single solid strands. Where additional flexibility is required such as halyards, 7x19 or 7x7 wire is used.

Other types such as Dyform, which is a variation of 1x19 with flattened strands, will occasionally be found, this being stronger for a given diameter. Rod rigging is rarely encountered on production boats. The key to rigging life is good articulation so each end of all wires must be free to move in all directions like a universal joint.

These days, rigging screws, or turnbuckles, are mostly made of stainless steel with chrome plated bronze bodies (which prevent the threads binding up under load which can happen with all stainless steel screws). They generally are very reliable but like all components in the rig should be very carefully examined for stress cracks or damage.

● SECTION 23, RUNNING RIGGING

- Wear, UV degrading? Think about chafe aloft which you cannot inspect with mast up. If the halyards etc have not been properly secured (known as frapped) then chafe is likely.
- Is it complete?
- General common sense sufficient.

Ropes now come in a large variety of types, some of which are very expensive. These are usually the very low stretch type and reinforced with fibres other than terylene and nylon. So if halyards of this type need replacement due to wear or damage, bear this in mind.

On very large yachts with mast(s) stepped, the survey will often include a trip aloft to inspect the entire rig, this sometimes carried out by a rigging company as an addition to the condition survey.

● SECTION 24, SAILS AND COVERS ETC

- Usually examined on board and not spread out. Use common sense and caution, this is a very subjective area. Also bear in mind type of vessel, a competitive club racer will have different expectations to a creek crawler. If in doubt suggest full inspection by sail maker in his loft. Be aware however that sailmakers will often consider old and worn sails as due for replacement when they still have some life left in them and make this point if you are writing a report. I once bought a boat some 23 years old and with her original sails. At the end of the season I took them to a sailmaker for washing and valeting, explaining that I knew the sails were tired but having just bought the boat I needed them to last a bit longer. He later phoned me and advised I should contact my surveyor because the sails had reached the end of their working life, I just said nothing and collected them. 5,000 miles and four years later I sold the boat and the new owner squeezed another three seasons of use out of the sails.
- Carefully check stitching chafe damage etc. Note however this is a random sampling only, not every seam can be checked without spreading the sails out. If you do this on grass etc bear in mind that any dirt etc they may pick up is your responsibility.
- UV degrading to headsails left on roller?
- Chafe damage to roller reefing mainsails due to friction?
- Roller headsails and mainsails are often examined set but beware of rocking the boat in her cradle; even in modest breezes serious damage can be done (which you would be responsible for).
- Beware description of sails. I once surveyed a large yacht described as having a 'spinnaker of cruising chute'. The sail on board for the survey was a nearly new cruising chute but when the new owner took the boat over he found this replaced with an old worn out spinnaker and legally there was nothing he could do. As an aside this is quite common with dinghies too, where the boat spec simply says 'inflatable dinghy' which of course covers the whole spectrum.

CHAPTER 10: **INSPECTION SECTIONS 25-30**

The next sub heading from the survey report covers sections 25–30.

● SAFETY

25. **Navigation lights**
26. **Bilge pumping arrangements.**
27. **Firefighting equipment**
28. **Lifesaving and emergency equipment**

Note ALL pleasure vessels proceeding to sea of 13.7 metres and above are subject to statutory requirements in terms of safety and lifesaving equipment, even when not in commercial use. The regulations can be found at:

www.mcga.gov.uk/c4mca/mcga-dqs-cvs-pleasure_craft_information_pack-web_document-3.pdf

Solas V also lays down some very basic regulations and requirements for smaller pleasure vessels, these also listed on the above site.

The Boat Data Book by Ian Nicholson and published by Adlard Coles Nautical is also a very useful source.

● SECTION 25, NAVIGATION LIGHTS

- Are the lights as fitted sufficient to conform to regs under sail and power?
- Are they type approved?
- Test if possible.

Full version of the Colregs including the lights and shapes required can be found at **www.boatsafe.com/nauticalknowhow/boating/colregs.html**.

● SECTION 26, BILGE PUMPING ARRANGEMENTS

- Are they adequate for the type of vessel? MCA Code is a good reference point, see **www.mcga.gov.uk/c4mca/mgn_280-2.pdf**.
- Do they work? (Test where possible.)
- Are strum boxes fitted?
- Check all pipework where accessible.
- With all systems ask yourself are there any circumstances whereby component failure etc could lead to water siphoning back into the vessel, particularly with owner fitted submersible pumps, the discharge of which might have been teed into another hose.

● SECTION 27, FIREFIGHTING EQUIPMENT

- Adequate for vessel? Most surveyors will adopt a particular code i.e. MCA Code of Practice or RYA guidelines and recommend equipment appropriate to vessel's area of operation. Do be sure to make a recommendation if equipment is inadequate because insurers may repudiate any claim arising from fire damage if inadequate.
- Are extinguishers still in date and if condition gauges fitted are these showing working pressure?
- All Halon extinguishers are now banned but many are still in service.
- Fire blanket at galley?

● SECTION 28, LIFESAVING AND EMERGENCY EQUIPMENT

- Adequate for vessel? Most surveyors will again adopt a particular code i.e. MCA Code of Practice or RYA guidelines and recommend equipment appropriate to vessel's area of operation.
- Is all equipment in date? Check external condition where appropriate.

A most useful website is **www.oceansafety.com**, particularly the downloadable safety checklists at **www.oceansafety.com/safetylists.html**.

The next sub heading from the survey report covers sections 29 and 30.

● ENGINE AND FUEL SYSTEM

29. **Engine and installation**
30. **Fuel system**

● SECTION 29, ENGINE AND INSTALLATION

- Most surveyors limit this to a visual inspection only. If you do this make sure it is a thorough inspection using extending mirror and spotlight. Look for cracked blocks, oil and water leaks, rusty hose clips, loose belts, cracks in exhaust injection bend. Give a general assessment of external condition. Keep a database of known issues with particular make/models.
- Check oil on dipstick and under filler cap for water contamination and emulsification of oil. If freshwater cooled, check in header tank for contaminated coolant. Oil analysis is sometimes offered by surveyors but in my opinion it is of little use without complete service records from new, as is the case where it is used in commercial applications.
- Some surveyors will briefly start engine if a water supply is available but remember engine cannot be put under load or be taken up to working temperature and this must be stated in report.
- Always look under engine even if only possible via an extending mirror or digital camera. Look for traces of oil or coolant in the bilges or engine tray. Are the bilges dry now? (having been 'prepared' for survey) but heavily oil stained from leaks?
- Record engine model and number where possible. Check this agrees with any details supplied.
- Exaggerated claims about engine maintenance and re-builds are frequently made, so ask to see invoices.
- Check engine beds and bearers, any movement, failure of bonding etc?
- Check engine mounts intact (rock engine or lift with crowbar). Where saildrive is fitted this can be flexed from under the boat to test the mounts.
- Check gearbox type and shaft coupling.

- Carefully inspect exhaust where accessible. Has it got a waterlock and gooseneck where necessary? (Waterlock to prevent water siphoning back into engine, gooseneck to prevent following seas entering system.)
  Note, all surveyors' professional indemnity policies now exclude any claims involving asbestos so note well any lagging etc in older engine spaces. Removal and disposal of any asbestos containing material would be at your expense if no warning is given.

Occasionally you will be asked to attend a sea trial in addition to the condition survey. Some surveyors will undertake this but it must be made clear that it is not a guarantee of mechanical condition. Below are typical observations:

- The engines started readily from cold without any excessive smoke.
- Both engines reached maximum continuous revs under way.
- When underway no fuming was noted in the engine space, and no leaks from the engine water, fuel and exhaust systems were evident.
- All engine instruments functioned, and oil pressure plus engine temperature at the gauges behaved normally.
- At the conclusion of the trial, after the engines had been stopped for 30 seconds they started immediately on tickover and immediately obtained correct oil pressure which was subsequently maintained without increasing revs.
- Ahead and reverse gears engaged normally.
- When each engine was run up to full revs under load individually with the other in neutral no excessive smoke was noted.
- It was noted that the water hose on the aft end of the small oil cooler on the port engine is beginning to perish. This is a heavy duty laminated hose not about to fail but it would make sense to replace it now.
- Both inboard shaft seals ran cold and no leaks were evident.
- No seepage from the rudder tubes was noted under full power with maximum squat aft.
- The steering operated correctly.
- Trim tabs operated under load.
- All electronics operated normally although not all functions were tested.

Conclusions

The sea trial did not indicate any serious faults with the engines and transmission, nor any other parts of the vessel.

Fig 121 shows a good example of information that can be gained by using a digital camera in spaces not accessible to view. This poorly marinised vehicle engine has been fitted with a pipe in the sump connected to a hand pump to change the oil. As can be seen the hose clip on this is about to disintegrate, resulting in loss of engine oil and probable catastrophic mechanical failure. Carrying out a thorough visual inspection and finding the less obvious things like this will greatly enhance your reputation and ensure your success.

Fig 122 shows typical corrosion and cracking seen in exhaust elbows. They corrode from the inside out due to the hot water and exhaust gases passing through them and should be regarded as a service item, but can be very expensive.

This is exactly the type of defect that a good visual inspection of the engine should identify. Due to poor access it is often necessary to use a mirror in conjunction with a powerful spotlight to fully inspect all parts. Video inspection scopes as described earlier are also very useful here.

Fig 121: Corroded clip on oil extraction hose.

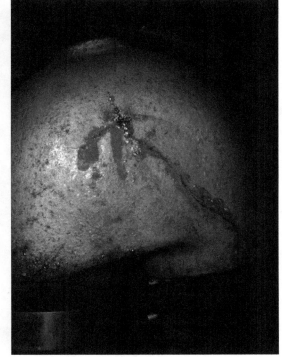

Fig 122: Corroded and fractured exhaust elbow.

Occasionally you will come across asbestos lagging still in place on older boats, as shown in Fig 123, and particularly those arriving from other countries where attitudes and standards differ from those in the UK. When the dangers of this material started to become known a common practice was to paint it over, this was deemed sufficient to contain any fibres. So always beware if you see this. Fig 124 was taken at the end of one of the exhausts in the same engine room, which is clearly a hazardous area and was immediately closed off.

Fig 125 shows a type of water filter very commonly used on engine cooling water intakes and there are thousands in use. The lid screws down and seats on a large rubber O-ring seal which can be seen in the top of the picture. Sometimes the lid can be cross threaded and this causes it to lock up without seating properly although it could give the impression to a person not familiar with such things that it is properly closed. If this happens the engine will draw air in here and overheat.

BUT

If the unit has been badly installed and not in accordance with the manufacturer's instructions and is below the waterline, then the boat will quietly sink if left unattended. I know of one very expensive yacht where one of these lids was cross threaded as described above but did not cause a problem at the time. Later, however, her large tanks were filled with fuel and water, which added just enough weight to put this unit a few mm below the waterline, and overnight she sank in her berth.

So always find some reference point and measure the height above waterline at which the unit has been installed. I also coded a new production yacht where the builders had fitted one of these in use on the generator some 8ins below the waterline in order to get it under a berth. And that was the builders.

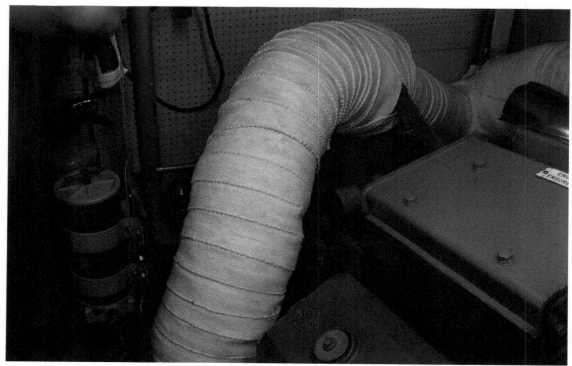

Fig 123: Asbestos lagging in engine room

Fig 124: Asbestos lagging with loose fibres and dust.

Fig 125: Standard cooling water strainer.

REPORT EXTRACTS

Very rusty fitting in base of sump

- Engine: Access is generally good. The diesel engine is a marinised BMC 4 cylinder unit. Engine found in reasonably clean external condition with no obvious leaks or serious external corrosion. Cooling is via indirect closed circuit heat exchanger system utilising standard Bowman components. It was noted that a pump is provided to remove the sump oil via a hose fitted in the base of sump under the engine. The fitting in the sump is of mild steel and very rusty indeed, as is the securing hose clip. Any serious leak here will cause the engine to lose oil with very serious consequences. Access is very restricted and it is considered essential this fitting be removed for full inspection. Video inspection scope can be used to examine inside tank if access via a dipstick for example is available. Clarity of fuel and presence of sludge in base of tank can be determined.

4.Recommendation: The steel fitting in the base of the engine sump to which the sump pump hose attaches should be removed for full inspection. The pump arrangement is poorly executed and it is suggested the whole assembly be removed and a standard oil extractor used via the dipstick.

General external condition of engine plus poor temporary repair to injection bend

- Beds: Of GRP moulded type and carried well fore and aft. No deterioration noted.
- Mountings: Of flexible type. These were examined with the engine running at tickover and were seen intact. Note: When the engine is driving the mounts are subject to considerable thrust and these conditions cannot be replicated ashore.
- Engine: The Thornycroft diesel is a 4 cylinder unit based on a 1.5 litre BMC engine. It was found in dirty and rusty external condition and there has clearly been a leak at the saltwater pump. All the steel hose clips are rusting and in need of replacement. Cooling is via indirect closed circuit heat exchanger system. Mechanical condition not established but the engine was tested briefly and ran smoothly. The most common fault with this engine is loss of compression and consequent poor starting but in this case the engine started readily.
- Transmission: The engine drives via a Hurth mechanically operated gearbox, this in good external condition with no obvious leaks. Gears were engaged briefly and operated normally. Spare RD type resilient coupling stored aboard.
- Controls: Of single lever cable operated type found in working order. Control box is recent.
- Exhaust: The cast iron injection elbow on the manifold is split and has been temporarily repaired with hose clips and plastic hose. The short copper pipe running to the injection bend is also corroded and suspect. The remainder of the exhaust is of flexible type and in serviceable condition where accessible. A gooseneck is fitted to prevent following seas entering system.

Recommendations: At the very least the engine should be serviced, the injection bend and pipe replaced, and all rusting hose clips renewed in stainless steel.
However this engine is believed to be the original and given that the boat is to be used for extended cruising, the better option would be complete overhaul or replacement.

General appraisal and notice of known issue

- Engine: Access is quite good with removable panels both port stb and fore and aft of the engine. The Volvo 2003 three cylinder diesel develops 28hp and is engine no: 2300027357. Engine in clean external condition with no obvious leaks. Oil on the dipstick and under the filler cap clean and free from any obvious water contamination.

There is a known problem with this model engine, (pre engine no: 2300059159, as in this case). In a few examples the spline drive between engine and gearbox has failed prematurely resulting in complete loss of drive. However the only way to test this is to separate the engine and gearbox to allow visual inspection of the spline. The older type as here can be modified and the broker's details state that this has been carried out, but no documentary was available at time of survey, this should be requested as it is a valuable record which should stay with the boat.

● SECTION 30, FUEL SYSTEM

- Material of tank. Beware mild steel sitting on wooden bearers or plywood panels. Examine as much as possible with extending mirror.
- Is tank secure?
- Is pipework copper or flexible type to BS EN ISO 7840? Is it well supported, not under stress and free from damage?
- Is a shut off cock fitted close to the tank and a pre-filter/separator fitted between tank and lift pump?
- Glass or plastic filter bowls and sight gauges are considered an unnecessary fire risk by today's standards but are still in common use. Sight gauges should at least have an isolating cock at the base which should be kept turned off when not reading the gauge. All filters in the engine space should have metal bowls, plastic or glass is acceptable if located outside of the engine space.
- If a petrol inboard engine the entire system must be exemplary. All insurance underwriters will expect the system to conform with one of the standards whether that standard is mandatory for the vessel or not and that is the sensible approach.

The MCA Code of Practice simply prohibits all petrol inboard installations, for both main engines and generators. The Boat Safety Scheme has a checklist for petrol inboards and it is suggested that be used.

- In small boats with petrol outboards (and larger craft which carry petrol for a generator or tender), be very aware of the storage arrangements, and any hazards when transferring fuel to any tank integral to the engine etc. One often encounters battery isolators and electrical switches that are not spark protected in areas where petrol vapour could conceivably collect. With petrol in particular the survey should be as much about risk assessment as condition.
- The Boat Safety Scheme now includes LPG as an engine fuel and when encountering this it is sensible to use that standard. It is also a good source of general information in arriving at a surveying standard for vessels not required to conform to any mandatory code.

REPORT EXTRACT

General description of fuel system

The steel tank is securely mounted under the cockpit sole. There is some surface rust to those parts of the tank that were readily accessible but when this was scraped away and the tank hammer tested it was satisfactory. The remainder was examined as far as possible via an extending mirror and no weeps or diesel stains were noted and as far as I can ascertain with the tank in situ the rusting is not serious. It would be possible to pressure test the tank in situ but it is suggested it be removed for full inspection as convenient. Particular attention should be paid to those parts of the tank that rest on the bearers where moisture will be retained, this promoting rust.

Delivery tubing is copper with some recent armoured flexible fuel hose within the engine space. A shut off cock is fitted at tank, and the fuel filtration provided is well above average. It was noted that the clear bowl of the primary filter is dirty, this should be cleaned and the element replaced. (Access is good in the locker under cockpit sole.)

System conforms to the general standards prevailing when vessel was built. No specific hazards were identified and system considered fit for use.

CHAPTER 11: **INSPECTION SECTIONS 31-37**

The next sub heading from the survey report covers sections 31–37.

● ACCOMMODATION AND ON BOARD SYSTEMS

31. **Accommodation, general**
32. **Gas installation**
33. **Fresh water tanks and delivery**
34. **Heads**
35. **Electrical installation**
36. **Electronic and navigation equipment**
37. **Heating and refrigeration**

● SECTION 31, ACCOMMODATION GENERAL

- During your detailed inspection of the interior during the survey take in the general condition of the interior.
- Open up as much as possible and look in spaces not inspected for years using extending mirror where necessary. Remember out of sight out of mind rules with many owners.
- Give a general report on cleanliness, condition of linings, furniture, bulkheads, upholstery etc.
- Some surveyors give a detailed description of the layout etc but this only necessary on request of client. The same applies to special requirements i.e. if the boat is to be used for serious offshore cruising are there adequate handholds, is cooker gimballed, are there seaberths? (Probably no to all of this in most production boats.) Talk to your client and ascertain his requirements.

● SECTION 32, GAS INSTALLATION

At the time of writing this is a most difficult area for surveyors and boat buyers/owners alike. There is an EU wide standard and a British standard which are not identical, and the vast majority of boats in use on the coast for pleasure do not have to comply to any standard whatsoever. It is stressed that the subject cannot be adequately learnt from a few pages in this book and further personal research and reading is essential.

So who can do what?

Only qualified personnel on the Gas Safe Register (CORGI prior to 1/4/09) can carry out full inspection and testing. It is thus worth a surveyor getting the relevant qualification for installations in yachts and small craft and obtaining registration. In addition Boat Safety Scheme Inspectors carry out testing and inspection, and those approved by the MCA to carry out coding of vessels in commercial use carry out inspections when coding boats. MCA and BSS requirements are broadly in line with the British and EU standards, BS 5482-3:1999 or ISO 10239:2000.

In practice however the majority of surveyors are not on the Gas Safe register or are not Boat Safety Scheme examiners, and many simply exclude the gas system from the survey.

So which boats are subject to what mandatory standards?

1. Boats in use on the Inland Waterways are subject to the Boat Safety Scheme.
2. Seagoing pleasure craft in commercial use and subject to the MCA Code of Practice.
   If the vessel falls into either of the above categories she should have current documentation aboard as described in chapter one, and the gas system will have been inspected as part of that regime.

3. Boats subject to the Recreational Craft Directive (i.e. the vast majority of production boats you are likely to encounter built since 15 June 1998) and CE plated as described in chapter one will have been built or post certificated to the RCD which contains the EU gas standard. Note however that as with all RCD criteria and as explained in chapter one, there is no requirement to stay in conformity after the vessel is first sold, so the gas system could have been changed or additional equipment installed.

What this all means is that a very large number of vessels surveyed on the coast are not subject to any mandatory regulation or standard.

What can we actually do?

- If the boat is subject to the BSS or MCA Code, then the system has been assessed to those standards. Confirm certification aboard.
- If the boat is subject to the RCD she would originally have complied with the EU standard. So check for any obvious damage, modification or additional equipment.
- If 1 or 2 above do not apply then the boat has never been required to conform to a particular standard, and is not required to now. At this point a surveyor has the option to survey the system to one of the standards but is it right to impose this on a system that is not required to conform? After all, non compliant systems are not automatically dangerous.

At the time of writing there is no standardisation and little guidance in the surveying world on this important topic. What follows is my own method, which I believe offers a sensible and responsible approach.

As described above firstly establish what if any category the boat falls into and comment accordingly, then the following standard wording is used:

Irrespective of the above (i.e. whether boat is BSS or MCA coded or not) ALL gas systems are subject to the checks listed below as part of this survey. Recommendations will be made where there is an obvious serious safety issue and these must be carried out before use. Suggestions will also be made where appropriate to enhance safety criteria, particularly with systems where there is no mandatory requirement to conform to a standard. It must be understood however that some insurance companies require a declaration from the assured that the gas system conforms to current standards, and if that is the case here upgrading will be required as a condition of the insurance policy.

Sources of further information include **www.calormarineshop.co.uk/rules-regs-answer.htm**. This gives comprehensive information on standards and best practice. Also, **www.boatsafetyscheme. com** contains much sensible advice and a helpful manual can be downloaded, even if your boat is not required to comply with the standards in it.

The following table lists inspections carried out in a typical condition survey. An example of this table in use can be seen in the full survey report which is part of the final chapter.

Additional observations

List any other points here, it is sometimes necessary to expand on the comments made in the above table, see example in final chapter.

ITEM	RESULT		ACTION REQUIRED. (R) Recommendation to be carried out before use. (S) Suggestion only.
Condition and efficiency of self draining bottle storage			
Age and condition of flexible hose			
Age and condition of regulator			
Condition of copper tubing where accessible			
Is tubing adequately supported and not under stress where accessible?			
Are all appliances fitted with flame failure devices on all burners, and did these work properly under test?			
Are any appliances requiring flues properly fitted with same?			
Is a gas alarm fitted?			
Is each appliance fitted with an isolating tap			
If fitted did leak bubble tester function?			

Further standard wording

The appliances were briefly operated and no obvious leaks were evident.

Please note however this survey is not any kind of gas safety certificate, that is only obtainable after comprehensive pressure testing and assessment by a qualified person listed on the Gas Safe Register (formally CORGI) **www.gassaferegister.co.uk**.

Note above the use of the word 'operated', as opposed to 'tested'. Testing in this context means full pressure testing of the system and that has not been carried out.

Some clients will be satisfied by the depth of inspection carried out here while others will commission a full test by a registered person.

Do be careful when inspecting gas systems to distinguish between the high and low pressure sides, basically if the regulator is mounted remotely from the bottle then everything bottle side is high pressure. These require different types of tubing and are subject to different criteria, for more information refer to the BSS manual.

You may decide to add more inspections to the above list and an excellent source for this is the Boat Safety Scheme manual. You may even decide to survey all systems to that standard. As I said back in chapter one, the surveyor is often left with the weighty responsibility of setting a standard for surveying to and gas systems are one of the prime examples. However using the method described above we have at least achieved four objectives:

- The setting out of clear and succinct information for the client as to what applies to the particular vessel in terms of standards and the potential insurance situation.

Fig 126: Perished gas hose.

- The imparting of sources of further information and advice.
- Carrying out of a series of inspections and recording the results, together with advice for enhancing the safety of a particular system.
- Established that the various appliances are operative.

We have thus fulfilled the responsibility of setting a standard for surveying to (where one doesn't exist) and this is infinitely better than simply excluding the system or giving some general description. It is an area though that is subject to change and most surveyors would welcome regulation and clarification.

Always bend the flexible hose when inspecting it. The cracks seen in Fig 126 are not easily visible until the hose is flexed. All hoses should be marked with the BS or ISO standard, and date of manufacture or date to be replaced by. Hoses on sale in the UK will normally be marked with date of manufacture but those from France for example will have a 'replace by' date. So be absolutely sure which you are looking at.

Fig 127 shows the obvious kind of deterioration one will often find but it is also a sign of the current Owner's attitude to the condition of his gas system and it should receive considerable scrutiny. This is inside the boat behind the cooker so any leak will be directly into the accommodation. The hose clip is close to failure and right by a test point, so the system has clearly not been tested in recent years or the clip would have been replaced.

This is also an indication of a general attitude to maintenance, particularly those out of sight out of mind situations. So on this boat you should be particularly vigilant and go to considerable lengths to inspect parts of the vessel not readily accessible.

Fig 127: Corroding clip on gas hose.

Fig 128: Very poor gas installation.

Fig 129: Very old corroded regulator.

This situation illustrated in Fig 128 is very commonly encountered, particularly inside gas lockers. The copper tubing is totally unsupported and very vulnerable to fracture. Each time the bottle is changed the copper is flexed and fatigued a little bit more.

The tubing should exit from the top of the locker but in this case it exits at the base and is not even sealed, nor is the adjacent electrical wiring, which should not be running through the locker.

Ferrous fittings are rusting and the copper tube is pitted. Where copper tubing is not clean and bright it should be gently scraped to determine the level of any pitting.

In a case like this where so much is obviously wrong with the accessible parts of the installation it is of course right to simply condemn the system and recommend replacement.

The system in Fig 129 was in use up to survey and the Owner complained he could smell gas. The regulator may well have been on Noah's Ark and the sealing washer and seating could not possibly function properly.

● SECTION 33, FRESH WATER TANKS AND DELIVERY

- Material and type of tank, condition and security? Beware of galvanised mild steel tanks sitting on timber bearers.
- Built in GRP tanks whereby the water is in contact with the hull moulding not recommended due to possible long term damage to laminate. On older boats suggest the top is cut out and a flexible tank inserted into the space.

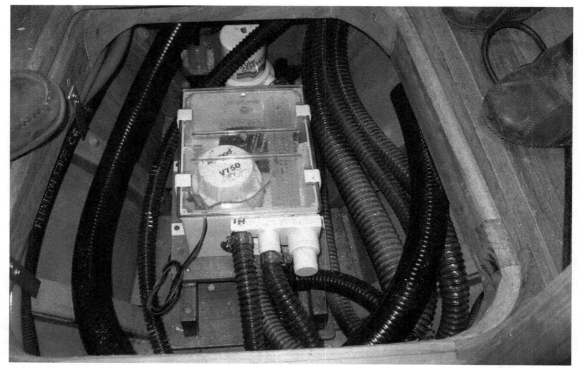

Fig 130: Grey water collection tank and pump.

- If GRP moulded tank, look inside for osmotic blisters if possible. This is very common, sound a warning about drinking water contaminated with traces of glycol, styrene etc.
- Condition of all hoses, clear type will allow light to enter promoting bacteria, algae growth etc. Should be of food quality but often are not.
- Test all pumps. If water foul when run off suggest sterilisation and flushing.
- Does any shower discharge overboard or into bilges?
- Overboard discharges should be dealt with in section 13.
- If grey water tank fitted, test associated pump/float switch if possible.
- If calorifier fitted check for corrosion and leaks around the 230v immersion heater unit and report any found with a warning.

Fig 130 shows a common arrangement whereby multiple discharges from sinks, showers etc are brought together in a small tank containing a float switch operated electric pump, thus avoiding multiple through hull discharges. It can simply be tested by running water in one of the sinks etc and checking for correct operation of the pump. Check that there is nobody, particularly the owner, under the boat first.

With all these systems check for any modifications or owner fitted equipment and examine everything with the overriding thought, is there any possibility that component failure etc could cause seawater to siphon back into the boat and flood the vessel. This is particularly the case with electric bilge pumps in grey water collection tanks like that in Fig 134, which may have been teed into another discharge.

REPORT EXTRACT

Rusted water tank covered up

Twin mild steel tanks are located under the cockpit sole. The tanks are well painted but when the underside of that to port was examined via an extending mirror some rust was noted close under the shut off cock. When this was examined by touch my finger went straight through the tank, the base at this point being completely rusted.

Recommendation: The port hand water tank is rusted through and in need of replacement. That to stb should also be removed for full inspection. Removing the tanks will be very time consuming and it is suggested a quote for the work be obtained prior to purchase of the vessel.

● SECTION 34, HEADS

- Common sense approach is sufficient.
- All through hull fittings will have been dealt with in section 13 Skin fittings etc.
- General condition and is unit secure?
- Do hoses have goosenecks or siphon breaks? If not sound warning. The MCA Code has a stipulation that if the rim of the toilet bowl is less than 300mm above deepest (i.e. loaded) waterline then anti siphon measures must be fitted.
- Check any holding tank system. Is any deck discharge fitting clearly marked?

● SECTION 35, ELECTRICAL INSTALLATION

The electrical systems in modern yachts are extensive and complex, and in some cases are the subject of a separate inspection by an electrician. Within the context of a condition survey for pre-purchase or insurance the inspection will be limited to basics and testing where possible. As with other items, if the boat is subject to the BSS, MCA Code or RCD then the installation will have been inspected (or installed) to the relevant standard and the same comments as per modifications etc as with gas systems apply.

Ships 12 or 24v system

- Are batteries secure and are isolating/changeover switches provided? Test batteries (simple no load voltage measurement). Are battery terminals covered and is adequate ventilation provided?
- Are all domestic circuits provided with dedicated fuses or circuit breakers of appropriate value? (Usually impossible to verify but give an opinion.)
- Heavy capacity items such as anchor windlasses should have a dedicated circuit breaker or fuse unit.
- General quality of installation? Tinned wire should always be used in marine installations but often is not.
- Battery charging provision? (Engine, solar and wind.) Is a 'smart' regulator system fitted to optimise charging? If maximum alternator charging output exceeds 2kw, MCA Code requires dedicated ventilated battery stowage.

kw = charging voltage, 14v for 12v system, x regulated alternator output in amps divided by 1,000.

- Test as much as possible and give a general opinion of the condition and quality of the installation.
- With sailing yachts check carefully condition of through deck plugs and sockets or similar arrangements for mast electrics.

230v Shorepower supply

- Must have approved RCD the shore side of all circuits and appliances, plus dedicated circuit breakers of appropriate value for all circuits and appliances. If connected simple tests can be carried out with a socket tester, but this will be testing the marina system as well as the vessel's.
- There is much debate as to whether the 230v system should be grounded to the ship's 12v negative but establishing this goes beyond a general condition survey. If you have any reservations about the 230v system, unless you have specialist knowledge get it tested by a qualified 230v electrician or specialist marine electrician.

Much will not be readily accessible when the yacht is complete and after a few years of operating in damp conditions some deterioration is inevitable.

In particular. Once the boat is a few years old electrical gremlins will inevitably appear and this is often due to cabling running low down in bilges as in Fig 132. All boats will at some stage have water in the bilges and if any wiring is not 100% insulated and protected then intermittent faults are likely to occur. One of the most common defects seen in this respect is submersible electric bilge pumps fitted in the bottom of a pump well or bilge and wired up using open chocolate-block type connectors, these only a few inches above bilge level. So even with a relatively small amount of water in the boat the connection will be submerged and the pump inoperative just when it is needed most.

Fig 131: Electrical system being installed in a new boat.

Fig 132: All this wiring will be submerged with very little water in the bilges.

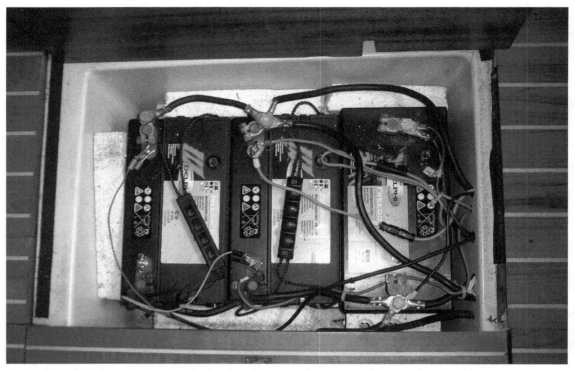

Fig 133: These batteries are well wedged in place but without securing straps would not survive a knockdown.

Fig 134: Typical 12v installation with main distribution panel, switches and fuses. This is a fairly simple 32' foot yacht and even at this level the wiring is extensive.

Fig 135: Good access and neat installation.

Fig 136: Through deck plugs and sockets at base of mast.

The plugs etc as seen in Fig 136 are obviously vulnerable to the weather and damage so need careful inspection. Very occasionally current leakage from mast electrics can be the cause of rapid corrosion in aluminium spars particularly at the heel with a keel stepped mast so if you came across such bear this possibility in mind particularly if it is accompanied by malfunctions in mast lights and mast associated instruments. Radar scanners are also heavy consumers of power and usually located on the mast.

During your inspection remove all the deck plugs if possible. If these are bound up with self-amalgamating tape, you will need the owner's permission first.

It is fair to say that modern deck glands etc are excellent but it takes a diligent and patient person to assemble them properly. These often get connected as everyone is rushing to launch at the beginning of the season and it is inevitable that the best job is sometimes not achieved.

If you are looking at a boat laid up and exposed to the weather with the mast unstepped do make absolutely sure that all sockets, glands etc have been properly sealed up because if they have been left open to the rain considerable damage may have been done to the sockets and wiring, resulting in costly replacement.

Fig 137 shows a typical shorepower installation in the engine space on a Dutch built boat. The vessel is pre-RCD but the installation fulfils basic safety requirements and is well organised.

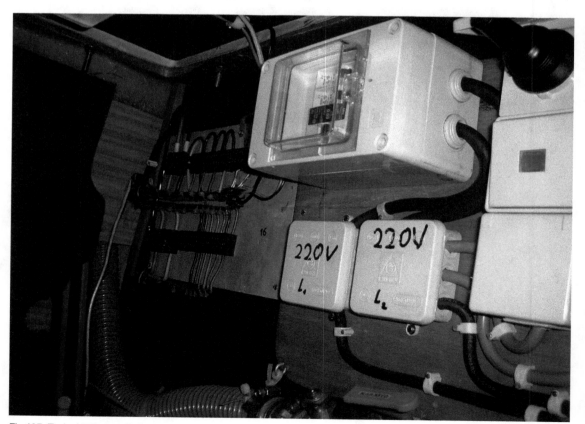

Fig 137: Typical 230v installation.

REPORT EXTRACTS

Typical system on an older boat not subject to any mandatory standard:

12v

The batteries are arranged in two banks, with three of about 110ah capacity under the berth in the port aft cabin, plus another bank of two under the berth in the stb cabin. All are well secured in place with terminals covered.

All were found in a badly discharged state, showing between 10 and 11 volts on test, but this dropped rapidly when a load was applied. Given that this boat has large capacity solar panels and a wind generator it is surprising to find all the batteries so discharged. I was unable to establish quite how these are wired but their capacity is certainly capable of keeping two of the batteries well charged for use as prime movers. It is most likely that the batteries are defective and will require replacement.

A master/changeover switch is provided in the aft port cabin. A 230v automatic battery charger/monitor is installed.

Wiring generally found satisfactory but not the tidiest installation. As far as could be ascertained all auxiliary circuits have independent circuit breakers or fuses. It was only possible to test the nav lights, water pump, bilge pump and interior lights before the voltage dropped too low. The central light in the saloon and that to stb aft were not working at time of survey.

230v

A basic 230v shorepower supply is provided but I was unable to locate either a primary RCD unit or dedicated circuit beakers for the appliances or ringmain, this must be verified. The 230v electrics were not tested and this system should not be used until its safety has been verified.

An older system added to on an ad hoc basis

No batteries aboard at time of survey but a temporary connection was made to start the engine.

As far as I could ascertain a single battery stows close to the engine, this being the dedicated starter battery but with switch provision to supply the auxiliary circuits. Two further batteries stow at the aft end of the dinette, these supplying the auxiliary and fridge requirements. Provision is made to secure the batteries in place.

Isolating and changeover switches are provided but I was unable to establish the various combinations available for supply or charging.

As far as could be ascertained all the original auxiliary circuits are independently fused at the switch panel, but a good deal of wiring has been added over the years, this not in a tidy and logical manner. It was thus not possible to verify that all circuits are protected by fuses or circuit breakers of appropriate value. This is particularly important with the fridge and anchor winch which are of high consumption.

A portable solar panel of 20w output and manufactured in 2001 was found aboard, tested and found to be working. A socket is provided for this in the locker to stb of the helm position and a regulator was noted in circuit, but again the installation is most untidy. (This item is not listed on broker's inventory.) It was not possible to ascertain which battery is served by the panel.

● SECTION 36, ELECTRONIC AND NAVIGATION EQUIPMENT

- A common sense approach is sufficient.
- Test where possible and record. Verify against any inventory.
- General quality of equipment and installation. With most modern yachts a full appraisal of the instruments and interfacing is a time consuming activity and only basic functions would be tested in the time scale of a routine condition survey.

● SECTION 37, HEATING AND REFRIGERATION

- Test where possible and record. Any gas appliances should be included in the section dealing with the gas installation.
- Very old catalytic type gas heaters contain asbestos so if unsure err on the safe side.
- General quality of equipment and installation. Adequate air gap around heater where applicable?
- Be particularly aware of exhaust gases discharging to atmosphere. Note flues discharging into open cockpit (or to the deck close to cockpit) may be dragged back into the accommodation if a cockpit canopy (as common on many motor cruisers) has been fitted. This particular scenario is not uncommon and fatal accidents have occurred because of it.
- Pay particular attention to solid fuel stoves, these cannot be tested during a condition survey and may leak in use. Never forget that fatalities with this type of stove are quite common, particularly where inadequate ventilation is provided.
- Check arrangements for flue cooling or insulation where it passes through deck. The traditional well deck flange is not much seen now but works very well.
- Establish what powers fridge. Some units can run on 12v, 230v and gas. Test if possible.

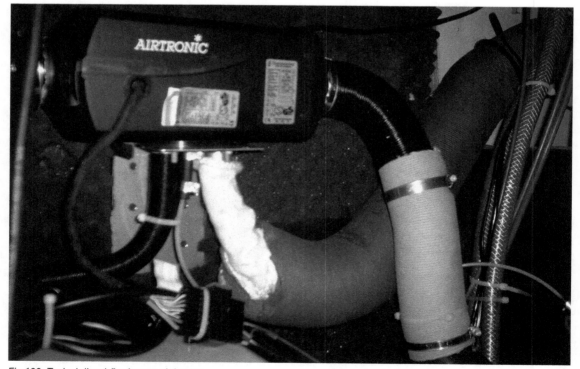

Fig 138: Typical diesel-fired warm air heater.

Many of the units illustrated in Fig 138 are owner fitted and not always to manufacturer's instructions. One important thing to remember is that the exhaust gets very hot indeed, hot enough to ignite flammable items close by. In this case the exhaust is lagged with glass fibre insulation where it comes out of the heater base, then continues into a large diameter insulated conduit which runs to the exhaust skin fitting. So always check the entire length of the exhaust.

REPORT EXTRACT

Faulty heater

An Eberspacher D3L diesel-fired heater unit is fitted. This was seen running for some time and fumes were detectable in the aft cabin and galley area. It is thus suggested that it be checked by an accredited installer or engineer familiar with this equipment before further use. The flue, although lagged, is fixed to a bulkhead and this should also be checked with the installation instructions. (Some filler has been applied to the opposite face of this bulkhead in aft cabin directly under the heater, as though some previous heat damage had occurred.)

So that concludes the onboard inspection during which we have collected a large amount of information and covered a great deal of ground. If you have been around boats for a while you already knew much of it (and may know a good deal more) but you have probably never tried to organise it into a formal inspection regime, nor record it in a methodical manner.

In the next and final chapter we will look at organising the information in a survey report.

CHAPTER 12: **SURVEY REPORTS**

TYPES OF SURVEY

This book is based around a Pre-Purchase Survey but below is a brief description of survey types commonly encountered:

1. Pre-Purchase Survey: This is self explanatory, a comprehensive survey commissioned by a potential buyer prior to purchase. The report will also be used by any finance house involved and the client's insurance company when he comes to insure the vessel after purchase.

2. Insurance Survey: This is a survey commissioned by the owner of a vessel when his insurer has requested a survey prior to renewing an existing policy. Typically these are required when the vessel is 20 years old and every 5 years thereafter, although criteria vary.

3. Damage Survey: This is a survey commissioned by an insurance company when a vessel they insure has suffered loss or damage. Criteria required by the insurers will vary case to case but there will usually be an additional investigative element.

4. Code of Practice Survey: This is an inspection to determine whether a vessel complies with various mandatory MCA Codes of Practice. This will typically be commissioned by the vessel's Owner or Agent where the vessel is being used commercially for charter etc. Most of the surveying organisations such as YDSA, IIMS etc are approved by the MCA to carry out these inspections and they nominate surveyors of suitable experience for the work.

5. Boat Safety Scheme Inspection: This is a similar to the above insofar as it checks the vessel against a given set of standards but is undertaken by approved BSS examiners who in many cases are not also marine surveyors.

6. Acceptance Survey: This is a comprehensive inspection of a new vessel carried out on behalf of her eventual Owner and usually involves sea trials.

7. Tonnage Survey: This is not a survey as such but a simple calculation based on a few measurements and is a requirement for British Part 1 Registration. Again various organisations are approved for the work.

8. Valuation: Again this is not a survey but a brief limited inspection based on strictly defined assumptions to provide a Value. This is usually Market value but other valuations are sometimes specified ie for a 'distress sale' where an immediate sale is required.

Such an inspection would typically include wording to the effect that:
'this valuation is not a survey and is based upon the assumption that a full condition survey would not reveal any major defects substantially affecting the boat's value'.

REPORT WRITING IN DETAIL

The report writing function of a surveyor is as important as the actual survey inspection. However technically gifted and experienced a surveyor may be, if he cannot express his findings accurately and in a manner that can be understood by his client, he will fail. Worse still if his reporting is not of the highest standard he may find himself being sued. Just being right will not guarantee immunity, one has to express everything in a manner that can be defended when under attack by legal professionals who will place an entirely different interpretation on your words.

A good example of this can be found in the conclusions of many survey reports on wooden boats which may say: 'This survey has found the vessel to be in sound structural condition', or words to that effect. This may seem a perfectly reasonable comment at the culmination of a defect free survey but consider the following scenario:

- The well built 35 year old vessel is surveyed without any major defects being identified and the above comment is made in the report conclusions.
- A few weeks after the sale has been completed the vessel is involved in a collision that damages the deck edge and top strake. The boat is taken to a yard for survey by the insurance company's surveyor who assesses the damage but also finds rot in the plywood deck, top strake and deckbeams, all this now revealed by the damage and some preparatory dismantling by the boatyard.

During the above process what we may term 'boatyard syndrome' kicks in. What this means is that the yard (quite rightly) wish to adhere to best practice in carrying out the repairs, after all it is their reputation that is at stake and their work that will be on show. So they may wish to investigate other related parts of the structure before carrying out the repairs in order that all potential risk of future deterioration is minimised, and that investigation may involve expensive dismantling. They may also suggest repairs that are of a higher standard than the original construction in order to prevent some potential defect developing. So the owner finds himself liable for a good deal of expenditure over and above the insurance claim which is limited to repairing the specific damage. At this point someone suggests making a claim against the surveyor and when this occurs, despite being somewhat aggrieved, the surveyor feels safe in the knowledge that his normal Limitations Section says:

'I have not inspected woodwork or other parts of the structure which are covered, unexposed or inaccessible and I am, therefore, unable to report that any such part of the structure is free from defect.'

This is a standard disclaimer as specified by PI insurers and one would expect it to disclaim liability for the above scenario. Wrong! Unfortunately the report also stated that the vessel was 'in sound structural condition' but in fact structural members were found to be defective when the vessel was damaged and subsequently dismantled. Now the legal arguments begin in earnest and even if the claim is eventually dropped it will typically take 12 months and considerable legal expenses to defend your position, and therein lies the rub. Most PI insurance policies in the UK now carry large excesses, typically £3,500 at time of writing, and this excess extends to defence of claims. So if after 12 months the claim is dropped it's a hollow victory if it has cost you £3,500 in legal expenses.

This has all been the result of inappropriate wording in the original report, and while that wording seemed entirely reasonable given the results of the survey inspection, a spin has been placed upon it by the legal profession which leaves you very exposed. The aggrieved party's legal representative will simply say that important structural members in the vessel were unsound at the time of the survey, but that your report conclusions specifically stated the vessel to be in sound structural condition, which it clearly was not. Your legal representative will counter by citing the disclaimer but this will probably not save you. The other side will say that if you could not inspect 'parts of the structure which are covered, unexposed or inaccessible' then you could not possibly state that the vessel was in sound structural condition and by doing so you have misled his client who specifically relied upon your statement, 'in sound structural condition', when purchasing the vessel at the agreed price.

In this example a more appropriate phrase might be: 'this survey has found the vessel to be in sound structural condition insofar as sufficient structural strength remains. However it should be appreciated that, given the nature of the material, dismantling may reveal some deterioration.' This is the reality for all professionals working in inspection and reporting regimes. So we must think very carefully indeed about how we express ourselves in any report and as emphasised in the preceding pages whether we are expressing opinion or fact.

Actually this is not as difficult or daunting as it sounds, provided you always remember to simply describe what you really mean and what you actually did, not just use the phrase that seems to fit conveniently. In the early part of this book we established four fundamental report writing principles which underpin this:

1. **Never confuse fact and opinion.**

2. **When a conclusion is drawn in a report as the result of a limited sampling that sampling MUST be fully defined in the report and it must be made quite clear that the conclusion is based on a limited sampling.**

3. **Areas that could not be accessed for any reason must be defined.**

4. **Any documentation concerning improvements or repairs claimed for the vessel must be listed in the report and it MUST be stated whether this documentation was examined or not, and remember, it's Invoices, not quotations you need to see.**

THE PRE-PURCHASE SURVEY IN DETAIL

For most surveyors in general practice the Pre-Purchase Survey provides the bulk of their work and that is what is described here in most detail, but the general principles apply to all reports.

The Pre-Purchase Survey is the most comprehensive of surveys and the report is a document upon which multiple parties rely, i.e.:

- The client in terms of whether he proceeds with the purchase at the agreed price.
- Finance houses in terms of whether they will lend money for the purchase.
- Insurance companies in terms of whether they will insure the vessel and at what premium.

So the surveyor's role is crucial and his exposure at its maximum. There is no room for vague or inaccurate reporting and the entire procedure must be conducted with complete professionalism.

- **Most common scenarios:** The most common scenario will involve a broker who will have arranged the potential sale and by the time a surveyor is appointed a 'subject to survey' contract will have been signed and a 10% deposit paid. In fact most brokers will not allow a survey to take place until this stage has been reached, but this is not set in stone. A less common scenario is a private sale where no agent or broker is involved and buyer and seller are in direct contact. In this case it is common to find no deposit has been paid and no contract signed. Potential buyers in this situation often turn to their surveyor for advice and it is good practice to refer them to **www.ybdsa.co.uk** or **www.rya. org** where there is considerable information concerning purchase of second-hand yachts and various comprehensive publications available including contracts etc.

- **Initial contact and client relations:** Most enquiries these days come via phone and email and in this respect a website with as much information as possible about yourself and services offered is invaluable. An enquiry form for an online quote is also useful. At this stage it is vital to find out as much as possible about the potential client and his expectations and plans for the vessel. It is also useful to gauge the level of practical knowledge he or she might have. One of the problems surveyors face is that we don't know whether our clients are extremely experienced practical people capable and willing to undertake major repair or maintenance themselves, or perhaps very busy individuals who also don't even know how to open the bonnet of their cars! This reference to cars is no accident because some clients may initially perceive the survey as the parts and labour warranty they are used to getting when they buy a car.

Of course a client's background and expectations etc assume even greater importance where the vessel is likely to require work. What would appear as a trivial defect to a keen DIY owner who could rectify it in a few hours could appear as a serious problem demanding professional attention to a person with little or no practical aptitude, and that person may seek to hold you to account for making light of it.

Thus we can immediately see how useful this information can be and in its absence one should assume the client to be less than practical and having to pay professionals to undertake all but the simplest maintenance. I always ask my clients whether they are practical types and enjoy DIY maintenance or whether they prefer to leave this to professionals, perhaps because they are too busy. This kind of approach usually leads into a general discussion about their previous boats and experience and produces invaluable background information.

In this preamble one must never lose sight of the fact that we work in a leisure industry and buying a boat is a major event and source of great pleasure for our clients. This is our work time but it is clients' leisure time and it's up to us to make the process as pleasant as possible. We can be both objective and professional without being aloof and full of self importance, which is an unfortunate attitude sometimes adopted by surveyors. It is of course self evident that being pleasant and helpful will generate more work.

Survey contract

It is strongly recommended that a pre-survey contract be agreed and signed prior to the job. This contract should at least state the purpose and extent of the survey, the agreed fee and the time scale for payment. Any contract used should be approved by your PI insurers. All of the surveying professional bodies have sample contracts and it is obviously sensible to use one of these.

In reality however many surveys take place after simply agreeing the basics by phone or email but if you do the job properly subsequent problems will be rare. This approach is not recommended however.

Report layout

Your report has two audiences with entirely different requirements, and it should be composed to suit both.

The commissioning client requires a comprehensive report on the vessel and all her gear and will usually spend a good deal of time studying the content. However the report will also be used by any finance house lending money for the purchase and by insurance companies subsequently insuring the vessel. These latter two parties are only interested in the limited information relevant to their requirements and have to deal with hundreds of survey reports per week. So they require a short, easily accessible summary upon which they can make their commercial decisions. Some surveyors place this at the end of the report in the form of conclusions and a valuation while others include a summary at the beginning. It doesn't matter where this information is but it should all be grouped together and easily accessible.

This is particularly important with insurance companies who require their clients to have boats over about 20 years old surveyed every 5 years. In this situation their clients will often ask for the name of a suitable surveyor and if the insurance company has found your reports competent and user friendly in their commercial environment your name will be in the frame.

Recording of information

It is worth stressing again here that a report can only be as good as the efficiency achieved in recording the information during the survey.

Report content

Your report must obviously contain some basic essential information such as the Client and vessel details, date, time and location of vessel, purpose of survey, limitations and any special conditions affecting the survey. This last item is crucial. If the inspection was limited by any special circumstance this must be clearly stated. A common example of this would be: 'The survey was hampered by the large amount of gear and equipment stored aboard and it was not possible to empty all lockers etc within the time available.'

Moving gear etc around the boat is part of the job up to a point but we cannot do the impossible. If the parties involved do not properly prepare the vessel for survey it is not our fault, but the circumstances must be recorded. If you feel that a particular circumstance has badly affected your ability to do the job properly you should recommend further opening up or investigation.

Report style

There are of course an infinite number of variations here but as long as the basic information is accurately recorded and conveniently accessible, precise style is not important.

Some surveyors like to include a detailed description of the internal layout while others will limit this to comments regarding its condition. My own preference is for maximum technical comment and description concerning condition and construction of the vessel with minimal description of the obvious. I consider that my expert time is better spent dealing with items that may be considered specialist and outside the scope of an amateur buying a boat, that is after all what he is paying for. However, technical comment should be written in plain English in order that it can easily be understood by all.

Wherever possible include additional useful information. A good example of this would be sources of spare parts for obsolete or specialist equipment and in this respect you should maintain a database of useful sources. The inclusion of any helpful information over and above the basic survey will be most appreciated by your clients and will inevitably generate more work.

 The use of photos in reports is now commonplace and again there is no right or wrong way. What is beyond question however is that clients like photographs. My own preference is for photos of specific defects or important aspects of the vessel only but my attitude has been changed by reports produced on the IBTC training courses which inspired this book, which coincidentally makes its own very strong case for the use of pictures.

When I started out it simply wasn't possible to use pictures so easily and quickly, but were I starting now I would fully embrace such an excellent tool. I am indebted to surveyor and good friend, Bob Owen, for one approach I particularly like. When Bob carries out a survey he takes about 100 general pictures of the vessel in addition to any for specific technical use in the report. He then saves these on a CD which he sends with the report, and this is universally well received. It's an excellent method because the general informal pictures are separated out from the formal report where in my view they really have no place.

Report composition

As has been emphasised throughout this book, there will be two main streams running through any report: fact and opinion. Unfortunately in many reports there will be a third stream, fiction. Under this heading, mistakes in the basic description of the construction are commonly seen, i.e. describing a sandwich deck as being of similar construction to the (solid) GRP hull. Such inexcusable errors display a breathtaking lack of basic knowledge and care and inspire no confidence.

Once a general structure for the report has been created in template form, and the basic rules of composition understood, report writing is not difficult. It is simply a question of recording exactly what the inspection entailed (and of course what limited it) and recording its findings. The best surveyors devise as many practical tests as possible to be used during the inspection in order that as much as possible can be moved from the opinion stream into the fact stream, it's that simple. What this means in practice is that instead of stating that something 'appeared' in satisfactory condition we apply a test to it and record the findings. That test may be limited in scope but provided its limitations are defined in the report and it is obviously of use, an item previously in the opinion stream can be moved into the fact stream on the basis that it passed the defined test. Note well the phrase 'obviously of use'. If you use any test then that test must add something of substance in order that opinion may become fact. The examination of masthead by binocular described earlier is an example of an invalid test which will give the client a false sense of security.

THE GOLDEN RULE IS NEVER CONFUSE OPINION WITH FACT. THINK CAREFULLY ABOUT EVERY STATEMENT IN THIS RESPECT AND DESCRIBE THE LIMITATIONS OF ANY TEST OR SAMPLING USED.

The following is a straightforward Pre-Purchase report for a popular standard production yacht. Photographs are included here to illustrate and emphasise a particular point.

At the request of Mr X this survey was carried out on 2/1/2010 at Stonebridge Marina, Stonebridge, UK, the above named being a prospective purchaser of the vessel.

Limitations

- Where access is restricted by fixed panels, linings etc it was not possible to examine and I cannot say those areas are free from defects. However in this case all the saloon sole boards were unscrewed and lifted for full inspection of the keelbolts and centreline structure.
- This report has been prepared for the use of commissioning client and no liability is extended to others who may see it.
- In some cases it is not possible to detect latent and hidden defects without destructive testing not possible without owner's consent.

Scope of survey

- This is a Pre-Purchase Survey and its purpose is to establish the structural and general condition of the vessel. Where items of equipment have been tested this will be stated in the text.
- Please note that where reference is made to the condition in all cases this must be considered in relation to the vessel's age, for example 'very good condition' should not be taken to mean 'new condition'.
- A general inspection of the engine and installation will be made, and in this case the engine was briefly run. It was not possible however to bring it up to working temperature nor run it under load.
- Mast was stepped and the rig was inspected from deck level only.

Recommendations

These will not be made concerning cosmetic or other minor defects, although relevant suggestions may be made in the text. Recommendations will be restricted to those defects that should be rectified before vessel is used (or within a given time span if specified), and items that may affect insurability.

Recommendations will be highlighted for quick reference. The recommendations are contained in the body of report in order that they may be read in context, and are also listed as part of the conclusions at the end of this report.

Conditions of survey

Vessel was examined in a cradle and is believed to have been out of the water for several weeks. No special conditions affected the survey unless mentioned in the text.

Information is reported in the sections below, followed by conclusions and a valuation.

Hull, deck and structure

1. Details of subject vessel
2. Keel
3. Hull below waterline

4. Topsides above waterline including rubbing strake etc.
5. Deck moulding
6. Coachroof
7. Cockpit
8. Hull/deck join
9. Bulkheads and structural stiffening including internal mouldings

Steering, stern gear, and skin fittings etc

10. Rudder and steering
11. Stern gear
12. Cathodic protection
13. Skin fittings and other through hull apertures

On deck

14. Main companionway and other accesses to accommodation
15. Ports, windows etc
16. Pulpit, stanchions, pushpit, lifelines and jackstays
17. Rigging attachment points
18. Ground tackle and mooring arrangements
19. Other deck gear and fittings
20. Davits and boarding ladders

Rig

21. Spars
22. Standing rigging
23. Running rigging
24. Sails and covers etc

Safety

25. Navigation lights
26. Bilge pumping arrangements
27. Firefighting equipment
28. Lifesaving and emergency equipment

Engine and fuel systems

29. Engine and installation
30. Fuel system

Accommodation and on board systems

31. Accommodation, general
32. Gas installation
33. Fresh water tanks and delivery
34. Heads

35. Electrical installation
36. Electronic and navigation equipment
37. Heating and refrigeration systems
38. Tender

1. DETAILS

Subject vessel is a standard Example 48 class yacht designed by Alan Grange and built by Easterly Yachts UK in 1988, number 6 of the class. The design is known as a true blue water cruising yacht with excellent sailing performance.

LENGTH OVERALL:	14.63m
LENGTH WATERLINE:	12.68m
BEAM:	4.36m
DRAFT:	1.86m
DISPLACEMENT:	13,163kg
BALLAST:	4,990kg
REGISTRATION:	Vessel has full British Registry, (also known as Part 1 registry), Official Number: 123456, this visible in the lazerette locker. It was not established whether the registry is current.
RCD STATUS:	The vessel was first put into use in the EU prior to 15th June 1998 and is not subject to RCD requirements.
VAT STATUS:	Vessel is advertised for sale as VAT paid but no documents were examined.
LLOYDS HCC NO:	xxxxx

2. KEEL

The long fin keel is made of lead and bolted to the hull moulding with 25mm stainless steel studs arranged in pairs.

The keel itself has been faired with epoxy filler to provide a very smooth surface, this is intact other than right at the forward end where it has been damaged, probably by a grounding. The underlying lead is not badly distorted or damaged, and the loss of the fairing filler is not serious. Elsewhere the epoxy fairing is adhering well and in good condition.

It is suggested that this damaged area be ground out and repaired to prevent moisture creeping under the adjacent good filler which will eventually cause it to de-bond from the lead keel.

Fig 139 was taken from the port side and shows the damage right at the forward end of keel.

The hull to keel joint has been faired with hard filler and this is breaking away along part of the joint. This is not uncommon where two very different materials are joined and does not indicate significant

Fig 139

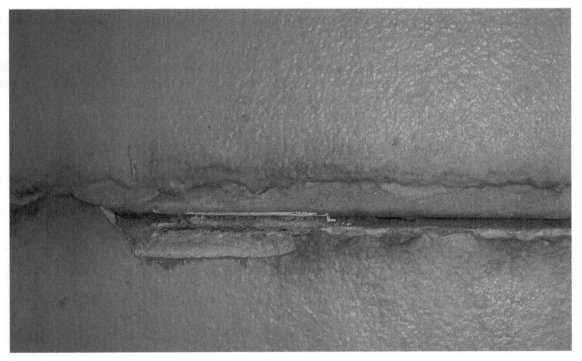

Fig 140

movement of the keel. Replacement of this fairing filler will probably be required annually although it is only applied to fair thr joint and reduce drag a little.

Fig 140 shows the port side of keel about 1 metre forward from the aft end. The underlying joint is tight and fair to the hull and that is the case along the entire length. The boat however was seen standing on her keel without the bolts being in tension. Very occasionally slight seepage may occur with lead keels, the material being relatively soft, and it can usually be cured by tightening the nuts a little.

Inside the boat it was noted that the 25mm diameter keel studs, nuts and backing plates consist of stainless steel of non magnetic austenitic grade. Where accessible all was found in good order with no significant corrosion noted.

The centreline is heavily reinforced by very substantial floors (heavy frames running across the keel root), these integral with the hull moulding.

The sections immediately aft of keel, (an area of high stress), are also slightly veed, this being inherently stronger than completely flat sections. No movement, stress cracking or failure of bonding noted throughout keel area where access was possible.

Keel attachment and associated reinforcing all found in good condition.

3. HULL BELOW WATERLINE

The hull below waterline is of FRP sandwich construction utilising a closed cell foam core.
Underbody generally found in good condition with no sign of major impact or repair.
No stress crazing evident around root of keel. Light hammer sounding did not suggest any delamination or voids.

There is some build up of antifouling but the old material is adhering well enough for overcoating. Moisture readings were taken over the hull using a capacitance type moisture meter of Sovereign Quantum type, operating in both shallow and deep reading modes. The meter was first checked for correct calibration. This meter has the capability to switch from shallow reading mode (3-6mm) to deep reading mode, (up to 30mm) whilst using the same scale. This is very useful in determining whether moisture has permeated to the core of a sandwich and the following procedures were used in this respect:

• The antifouling was removed in 30 areas around the underbody and readings taken on the underlying surface in both shallow and deep reading modes.
• The meter was then run over the entire underbody on the surface of the antifouling in order to identify any areas where readings were significantly higher than elsewhere. Particular attention was paid to areas around the through hull fittings.
• 50 readings were taken inside the hull below the waterline operating in both shallow and deep modes.
• 50 readings were also taken in the topsides well above the waterline in order to provide a comparison.

The readings recorded below are from the meter operating in the shallow mode on the relative scale 0-100 and taken in the 30 areas where antifouling was removed. When switched to deep reading mode there was no appreciable increase in the readings and this confirms that no further deep seated moisture is present. Please note there is no direct comparison with readings obtained with older type Sovereign meters.

The readings are relative and do not express moisture content as a percentage of dry weight. High moisture content is not generally a structural defect, and is to be expected in older boats. However where some moisture has been absorbed the likelihood of moisture related problems occurring is higher, and the actual state of the laminate cannot be completely guaranteed without destructive testing followed by chemical analysis.

The opinion given in this survey is based on all the evidence available at the time but without destructive testing.

The conditions prevailing when the readings were taken were as follows:

AIR TEMPERATURE:	11.9°C
SURFACE TEMPERATURE:	12.6°C
RELATIVE HUMIDITY:	65%

In summary, the weather conditions for obtaining moisture readings were good.

Readings were as follows:

METER	RANGE BELOW WATERLINE	RANGE ABOVE WATERLINE
Sovereign Quantum, Scale A, 0–100 Shallow mode	15-25, with the majority at the lower end of this range	13-14
Deep Mode	No increase	No increase

These values and the procedures described above indicate that some moisture has been absorbed but not to the core material. Given the age of the boat it is to be expected that some moisture would be absorbed through the gelcoat and into the solid outer FRP skin only but the levels found are not unduly high and no cause for alarm. They are also below the level at which the risk of osmotic blistering and other moisture related defects developing becomes significant.

In the 30 areas where antifouling was removed an epoxy coating was found, this believed to have been applied over the original gelcoat as additional protection against moisture ingress. The colour of the coating suggests it is of International Gelshield type. In all areas where the surface was exposed the epoxy coating was found free from visible defect and adhering well.

Epoxy coatings, gelcoat and sandwich laminate considered in good condition at this time.

4. TOPSIDES ABOVE WATERLINE INCLUDING RUBBING STRAKE ETC

The topsides are also of FRP sandwich construction. Light sounding did not suggest delamination or voids. No sign of major impact or repair evident.

No stress crazing or cracking noted in way of bulkheads or other internal reinforcing members. No damage noted in way of transom edge.

As described above, 50 moisture readings were taken around the topsides operating in both shallow and deep reading modes. In addition 20 readings were taken inside the hull and results obtained were entirely normal.

Topsides moulding found very fair and finished in the original white gelcoat. On the starboard side about 1m aft from the anchor locker drain and slightly below that line a small hollow can be seen in the topside under certain light conditions. The hull is entirely sound here and this hollow is most likely an original moulding characteristic. Some slight unfairness can also be seen below stanchion no 2 starboard side.

There is an area of UV degrading to the port topsides, this between stanchions 1 and 2. Here there are very tiny surface cracks in the surface which retain dirt. However this cannot be seen from 1 metre away and does not spoil the overall very smart appearance. Coating the topsides with a good quality wax polish containing UV inhibitors will help to preserve the appearance.

5. DECK MOULDING

The deck is of sandwich construction with end grain balsa core stiffening. Plywood is incorporated into the laminate in way of load bearing fittings and areas of high stress. Entire deck found firm underfoot with no sign of delamination or other structural defect. Hatches to the lazerette and gas locker aft secure and weathertight.

The entire deck area is laid to teak, this bonded in place thus avoiding screw fastenings piercing the top FRP lamination and providing a potential path for moisture to enter the core material.

The teak deck is stated as new in 2007. It was found adhering well and in good order with no serious wear, and with the paying (sealant) adhering well to the sides of the seams. On the stb quarter in way of

Fig 141

the pushpit base there is a split in the teak (Fig 141), this should be filled with thickened epoxy to prevent a piece being ripped out if it is caught on a sheet etc.

Those parts of the deck moulding not covered in teak were found in good condition with no serious wear, UV degrading or crazing noted.

6. COACHROOF

Integral with deck moulding and of similar sandwich construction. All found firm underfoot with no sign of delamination or other structural defect. No distortion or crazing noted in way of past aperture. Teak handrails secure. The horizontal surfaces are laid to teak, condition as per the main deck. The coachroof coamings (sides) and other parts where the gelcoat is exposed were found in good condition with no serious wear, UV degrading or crazing noted.

7. COCKPIT

Integral with deck moulding and of self draining type. There are no deep lockers open to the bilges, or lifting sole panels, this is a genuine self draining cockpit. The entire moulding was found in good order. No delamination noted to the cockpit sole and other high use areas. The horizontal surfaces are again laid to teak, condition as per main deck. On the starboard side just aft of the original sheet winch another split was noted in the teak (Fig 142).

This should be filled with epoxy as described in section 5 above to prevent it being ripped out if caught on a sheet etc. The wheel pedestal assembly all secure to the cockpit sole and in good order. Teak folding cockpit table in good order but requires scrubbing and varnishing. Lids to the two shallow lockers secure and in good order.

Fig 142

Due to the most of the horizontal surfaces of the deck, coachroof and cockpit being covered with teak no moisture readings could be obtained externally, and very few internally due to linings. However those obtained inside the boat were satisfactory.

8. HULL/DECK JOIN

This is of mechanical type consisting on two horizontal flanges through bolted via the toerail bolts. Access limited by linings etc. but where seen found in good condition with no sign of leaks.

Toerail of aluminium extrusion all lying fair with no signs of distortion due to collision. The section from stanchion 2 to the bow has been replaced and is in very good condition. Elsewhere the original toerail has some minor corrosion around the fixing bolts and some wear to the anodising, but all is serviceable for some years yet.

9. BULKHEADS AND STRUCTURAL STIFFENING INCLUDING INTERNAL MOULDINGS

A number of components contribute to the overall structure:
a)   The shell mouldings are robust in the first place.
b)   Primary bulkheads are well bonded into the shell mouldings.
c)   Secondary partitions are well bonded into the shell mouldings.
d)   Various frames formed over foam cores are utilised.
e)   The keel area is heavily reinforced with deep transverse floors as described in section 2 above.
(Floors are heavy transverse frames across the centreline but not continuing full height up to deck level).
f)   Fore and aft stringers of half round section are also incorporated into the shell moulding.
g)   A further deep and very robust FRP stringer runs behind the saloon berths to dissipate rig loadings.

The structure was examined wherever possible and no stress cracks, fractures or failure of bonding was noted.

10. RUDDER AND STEERING

External:
a)   The free standing rudder consists of a moulded blade around a substantial aluminium stock. No splits or weeps noted at edges of blade, and moisture readings on the blade are normal.
b)   No undue play in bearings present.
c)   No movement was detectable between the blade and stock when my full strength was applied to the blade with the steering hard over against the stops.
d)   The steering is correctly adjusted with rudder travelling equal distances port and stb.
e)   The rudder tube is believed to be of aluminium and where it emerges from the hull fairing filler has been applied. The filler has broken away in places and it would be prudent to make this good. Very little of the tube could be seen but the filler does appear to be protecting the aluminium rudder tube from potential corrosion and as such it has an important function.

Internal:
a)   Very little access was possible to the rudder tube, stock and quadrant inside the boat due to the large amount of heavy equipment stored in the lazerette locker, which I was unable to remove without help. However it could be seen that the mild steel clips securing the eyes in the ends of the steering cables were very rusty indeed. (Fig 143)

Fig 143

1. Recommendation: The clips securing on the eyes each end of the steering cables require replacement. It will be necessary to remove all the heavy gear from the lazerette to carry this out and opportunity should be taken to examine the entire assembly as this could not be carried out during the survey.

b)   Mild steel quadrant secure on stock but unable to test under load.
c)   The rudder tube is well braced where it passes through the hull.
d)   Turning blocks and cables visible in the engine room in good order and secure.
e)   The cables are provided with grease cups, these accessible under the seat in aft cabin.
f)   Wheel pedestal secure and in good condition. The cockpit sole is heavily reinforced at this point.

Advisory Note: given the age of this yacht and the miles she has covered it would be prudent to drop the rudder for examination of the aluminium stock for corrosion and cracks at the next opportunity. This would also allow better access for inspection of the rudder tube. At the same time the damaged fairing filler around the tube externally could be made good.

I do not consider this work to be essential now but should be part of the planned maintenance schedule. It should also be borne in mind that any application of the long lasting copper rich antifouling coatings popular today (such as Coppercoat etc) may promote rapid corrosion of the aluminium parts.

11. STERN GEAR

External:
a)   The fully feathering 3 bladed bronze prop was found secure on the stainless steel shaft. There is no damage or significant corrosion to the prop. There is quite a lot of wear in the mechanism but the unit still functions correctly. The original spare 2 fixed two bladed prop is stored under the seat in aft cabin, and found in good condition.
b)   Shaft is supported by a P-bracket, this aggressively tested, found secure and in good condition.
c)   The cutless bearing is badly worn and in need of replacement.

d)   Due to the large number of badly marked pots and nets around our coasts it is suggested a rope cutter be fitted.

e)   Shaft rotated by hand, found true with no binding of bearings noted.

Internal:

a)   Stern gland and seal: This consists of an old fashioned bronze stuffing box connected to the stern tube using a short length of heavy duty industrial hose, this secured both ends by 2x stainless steel hose clips. Hose inspected via touch and a mirror, no splits or damage noted. Clips tested and all holding well with no staining evident. The clips should be inspected regularly as serious corrosion to the back hidden surfaces of the clips is common, this identified in its early stages by heavy brown staining. Access to the stern gland is achieved by removing the bottom drawer in the chest of draws at forward end of the aft cabin. The gland is provided with a greaser for lubrication here. The gland has clearly been leaking a little which is usual with this type of installation. The standard multi lip type Volvo type seal provides a trouble free simple alternative to this old type seal.

b)   Stern tube seen secure in hull.

c)   Aquadrive thrust bearing and universal joint coupling securely fitted to FRP flanges integral with the hull, no movement or cracking noted.

> **2. Recommendation:** The cutless bearing requires replacement. Whilst this work is being undertaken the wear in the feathering propeller should be checked against manufacturer's tolerances.

● 12. CATHODIC PROTECTION

a)   Vessel fitted with a bar anode and electrical continuity between the anode and all the stern gear was confirmed. Anode part wasted but not yet in need of replacement. Mounting studs for anode secure. Not all of the skin fittings are bonded to this anode but this is not considered necessary.

b)   Shaft anode also fitted, this part wasted but not yet in need of replacement.

c)   Dedicated propeller anode fitted, this not yet in need of replacement.

System considered adequate

● 13. SKIN FITTINGS AND OTHER THROUGH HULL APERTURES

No skin fittings or valves were dismantled as part of this survey but the following routine tests were carried out:

a)   Examination from outside and inside the boat.

b)   All valves open and closed to their full extent.

c)   Any fixing bolts hammer tested where accessible.

d)   Bodies of the valves or seacocks tested with a hammer inside the boat and external parts hammer tested outside the boat.

e)   Fittings aggressively tested inside the boat for security in the hull.

f)   Hose clips inspected and hoses aggressively tested for security.

g)   Unless evidence to the contrary is found it is assumed that all ballvalves referred to below are made of Dezincification Resistant Brass (DZR) to specification DZR1 (BSEN 1982 CC752C). This is a special alloy for die casting and approved for use in the marine environment.

Accessible stb side of engine:

a)   Engine Intake consisting of bronze through hull fitting with a gatevalve and strainer, all satisfactory. The bronze strainer unit in good order and the wing nuts which secure the lid in place are free. There is

Fig 144

an intake for the salt water pump at the galley teed into this and the securing clips on the hose are very corroded. (The blue hose in Fig 144). These require replacement and condition of tee piece checking

b)　　　Cockpit drains consisting of a bronze Blakes seacock FRP bonded into hull, all satisfactory.

Accessible in aft heads compartment:

c)　　　Heads/holding tank discharge consisting of a bronze Blakes seacock FRP bonded into the hull, all satisfactory.

d)　　　Shower tray/sink discharge consisting of bronze through fitting with ballvalve, all satisfactory. (This is just above waterline).

e)　　　Heads inlet consisting of a bronze through hull fitting with ballvalve, all satisfactory.

Accessible under lifting trap at galley:

f)　　　Galley sink discharge consisting of a bronze Blakes type seacock FRP bonded into hull, satisfactory but requires freeing off.

Accessible under sink in forward heads compartment:

g)　　　Shower tray and sink discharges consisting of a bronze through hull fitting with ballvalve, all satisfactory.

h)　　　Inlet and discharge for heads consisting of bronze through hull fittings with ballvalves, satisfactory but discharge very stiff.

Accessible under forward berths:

i)　　　Port side believed to be inlet for deckwash consisting of a bronze through hull fitting and ballvalve, all satisfactory.

j)   Stb side discharge for holding tank consisting of a bronze through hull fitting and ballvalve. Valve seized and hose clips corroding.

k)   Log impeller housing and echo sounder transducer secure. (There is a small lifting trap to gain access to the log fitting just outside the forward heads compartment but it is necessary to unscrew the entire sole panel in the forecabin for access to the original through hull echo sounder transducer). These fittings are of plastic consisting of a large threaded body with an external flange and secured in the hull utilising a large plastic nut located on the body. Fittings secure and flanges intact but there have been a few incidents involving this type of fitting where the external flange has sheered off allowing the body of the fitting to come loose into the boat leaving a 1.5" diameter hole. This is rare but all unreinforced plastic such as this will deteriorate over time and the life of the fitting is largely dependent on the amount of tension it has endured since being fitted in the first place. Many installers over tighten these fittings and it is therefore prudent to apply a light GRP lamination or epoxy fillet over the securing nut and onto the surrounding hull surface inside the boat in order that the fitting remains in situ should the flange sheer off. Obviously the flange should be inspected whenever the opportunity arises.

l)   Various grounding plates bolted through hull, bolts hammer and screwdriver tested.

m)   Bowthruster secure..

Above waterline:

Two plastic and two bronze through hull fittings secure. The two plastic fittings are right aft on the stb side and the forward of these two fittings is not lying fair to the hull. (Fig 145). This is placing an unfair strain on the flange which may eventually shear off. The photograph below illustrates this and given that the fitting is only a few cms above the waterline it should be attended to. When replacing these old plastic fittings it makes good sense to use bronze, which are only a few euros more expensive.

3. Recommendation: There is an intake for the salt water pump at the galley teed into the engine cooling water intake and the securing clips on the hose are very corroded. These require replacement and condition of tee piece carefully checking.

Fig 145

The ballvalve for the forward holding tank discharge under forward vee berth requires servicing and the hose clips replaced.

The ill fitting plastic discharge right aft stb side just above the waterline is placing an unfair strain on its flange and is liable to shear. This should be replaced and it is suggested a new fitting of bronze be obtained.

14. MAIN COMPANIONWAY AND OTHER ACCESS TO ACCOMMODATION

a)   Forehatch is of aluminium framed perspex type, securely hinged with positive method of closure.
b)   Similar over aft cabin.
c)   Similar hatch over saloon.
The above are full size and suitable as escape hatches.
d)   Similar but smaller hatches for ventilation over both heads compartments.

All the above hatches are by Lewmar and in good condition throughout apart from some light crazing to the perspex. All sealing gaskets intact with no signs of seepage below. Hatches a), b) and c) can be opened from below and on deck.

e)   Main companionway access and hatch to aft cabin have sliding polycarbonate panels working in aluminium channels, and plywood washboards all in good condition. Hatchboards have lanyards to secure them in place from below.

15. PORTS, WINDOWS ETC

Vessel fitted with:
a)   6 aluminium framed fixed perspex ports. No significant crazing present to perspex, or corrosion to frames. Externally the frames are lying tight and fair to the coamings. The ports are secured by a nut and bolt (of internut type) in each corner with self tapping screws elsewhere. Some of the fastenings in the port in the aft cabin stb side forward are loose and require attention.
b)   8 opening Lewmar perspex ports with aluminium frames, all in satisfactory condition and gaskets intact. Some light crazing is present to the perspex but still of adequate strength. Full set of mosquito screens aboard.
From below no evidence of seepage in way of the above ports noted.

16. PULPIT, STANCHIONS, PUSHPIT, LIFELINES AND JACKSTAYS

a)   Pulpit: Of stainless steel, secure and in good condition.
b)   Pushpit: As above. Stainless steel support for antennae in good condition. The bolt which secures it to the pushpit is missing but it is still secure.
c)   Stanchions: Of stainless steel set in stainless steel bases all in good condition and secure but the stanchions are a loose fit in the bases. This is not a problem but the stanchions feel insecure when first grabbed.
d)   Lifelines: Of stainless steel wire and in satisfactory condition.
e)   Jackstays: Of terylene webbing and in serviceable condition. (Stored in cockpit locker).

17. RIGGING ATTACHMENT POINTS:
Vessel has a swept back double spreader rig with cap shrouds, intermediate shrouds, lowers, standing backstay, running backstays, masthead and ¾ forestays, plus a babystay.

Fig 146

a)   Main cap, intermediate and lower shrouds: These consist of stainless steel plates which pass through deck and are bolted to massive tie rods attached to a stringer bonded into the topsides and carried well down same. No sign of any movement or significant deterioration noted. There has been some past slight seepage around the chainplate on the port side but this of little consequence. Access to these vital components is straightforward behind the berths in main saloon.

b)   Main forestay: This consists of a substantial stainless steel plate passing through the stem with a captive backing plate running down the stem a very strong arrangement.

c)   ¾ forestay: This consists of a stainless steel plate bolted through the anchor well bulkhead. This can be seen in the anchor locker and the stainless steel nuts and bolts are heavily stained. Crevice corrosion may be forming and these should be replaced, (Fig 146).

d)   Babystay: This consists of a stainless steel plate through the coachroof, all secure.

e)   Standing backstay: These consist of a plate bolted through transom with backing plates in position, simple and strong. Base of transom is strengthened by a heavy knee integral with the moulding.

4. Recommendation: The bolts securing the ¾ forestay chainplates to the anchor well bulkhead should be drawn for full inspection.

18. GROUND TACKLE AND MOORING ARRANGEMENTS

a)   Main bower anchor: This is of Plough type of 22kg and in new condition. Anchor self stows with pin to lock it in place. Vessel is equipped with a long length of 10mm chain all in satisfactory condition. but please note this was not laid out and examined link by link. Bitter end attachment not examined.

b)   Kedge anchor: Also Plough type and about 16kg. Anchor has a suitable multiplatt warp and chain attached. (Stored in lazerette).

c)   Vessel has adequate cleats fore and aft, of adequate size and securely through bolted with reinforcing within the laminate.

d)   Cleats also fitted amidships for springs.

e)   All fairleads integral with the toerail in good order.

f)   Stemhead fitting incorporates twin rollers, these free and not worn, and fitting has provision for pin to prevent chain jumping in adverse conditions.

g)   Electric windlass securely through bolted and in good condition. In working order but not tested under load.

19. OTHER DECK GEAR AND FITTINGS

All found of adequate size and securely through bolted, although inspection from under limited by linings etc. Where accessible found with adequate additional reinforcing within the laminate.

The following winches are fitted, these all tested as far as possible but not under full load:

a)   Primaries: 2x Anderson 58 stainless steel self tailing electric type in good order.

b)   Secondaries: 2x Lewmar 55 self tailing type in good order. Some wear to the chromium plated barrel on that to port.

c)   For sail controls led aft: 1x Lewmar 46 and 1x 40 self tailing type in good order. All associated clutches and turning blocks in good order.

d)   For mainsheet : 1x Lewmar 43 self tailing type in good order.

e)   At mast: 2x Lewmar 46 self tailing type in good order.

None of the above winches have any excessive mechanical play.

Genoa tracks and cars in good order.

Ditto mainsheet track and traveller.

The turning blocks for the genoa sheets are in serviceable condition but the one on the stb side requires attention to one of the backing plates accessible in the locker in aft heads compartment. Here it can be seen that the aluminium backing plate has corroded away and requires replacement. This is also causing a small deck leak (Fig 147).

Fig 147

20. DAVITS AND BOARDING LADDERS

Vessel fitted with a stainless steel folding ladder securely bolted through transom, this in good condition. The ladder extends well below the waterline to when lowered to aid MOB recovery.

21. SPARS

Mast:
Well set up with a little pre-bend. As far as could be seen with mast stepped the Kemp silver anodised aluminium mast with in mast mainsail reefing is in good condition with no corrosion around fittings and rivets.

Seen from deck level both pairs of spreader brackets are lying tight to the mast. All fittings accessible from deck secure in good condition. No sail was in place and there was limited access to the mast reefing gear mechanism but where it could be seen it was found in good condition and free.

The mast boot was not removed and the mast could not be examined where it passes through the deck. It was also not possible to examine the mast heel without dismantling the saloon table and this was not carried out.

Boom:
The aluminium boom also found in good general condition. Some chafe damage to the anodising was noted close to the mainsheet take off point.

Rigid vang and associated gear all in good working order. No undue play noted in the gooseneck fitting.

Others:
Carbon fibre booming out spar in good condition.

22. STANDING RIGGING

Age not established. As far as could be seen with mast stepped the 1x19 stainless steel rigging is in good condition with no kinks or damage to the wire noted. All the terminals at deck level are of stainless steel type and no cracking to the terminals or staining was noted where the wires leaves the terminals. The lower terminals were electronically tested using the Kelvin four wire method and a Maidsure

Rigtester meter and the readings obtained were all within normal parameters with no indication of defect within the terminals. (The forestay lower terminals were not accessible with the reefing gears in place). It was noted that the top ends of the flexible wires up the mast all leave the rigid terminals in good fair lines which is essential to avoid premature fatigue.

The rigging screws of chrome plated open bodied bronze type were found free from visible stress cracks and distortion, and fitted with integral toggles to provide maximum articulation.
Facnor headsail roller reefing gear in good external condition and fitted with sufficient integral toggles at base to allow full articulation. Stated as new in 2008. No damage to luffspars evident seen from deck level. Harken reefing gear for staysail also in good condition as above.
Hydraulic backstay tensioner in working order.

23. RUNNING RIGGING

a)   Wire main halyard in good condition.

b)   All remaining running rigging is of terylene and in good condition.

24. SAILS AND COVERS ETC

a)   Sprayhood and stainless steel frame in good condition. Bimini in serviceable condition.

b)   Spinnaker contained in a snuffer and could not be examined.

c)   High visibility orange Dacron storm jib examined as far as possible onboard and in very good condition. (Stored under aft berth). Sail is damp and should be dried to prevent mildew developing. This item is not listed on Inventory.

d)   No other sails aboard at time of survey. Note the photograph on Broker's details shows the vessel flying a spinnaker but none is listed on the Inventory.

25. NAVIGATION LIGHTS

Vessel fitted with:

a)   Bicolour on pulpit.

b)   Stern light in working order.

c)   Steaming light.

d)   Tricolour at masthead.

e)   360 degree white at mast head.

All above tested and in working order. Vessel conforms to current regulations for this length overall under sail and power.

26. BILGE PUMPING ARRANGEMENTS

The bilge pumps could not be tested and their efficiency should be verified.

27. FIREFIGHTING EQUIPMENT

a)   1x 1kg dry powder extinguisher with condition gauge indicating working pressure. Halon auto heat triggered type within engine space. The use of Halon is now banned and this should be taken out of service.

b)   1x 2kg dry powder extinguisher with condition gauge indicating working pressure. This is overdue for service.

c)   Fire blanket at galley.

> **5. Recommendation:** The provision of fire extinguishers is not considered adequate and should be increased. The following is considered a minimum and is based on the requirement for a vessel of this size and type found in the MCA Code of Practice (**http://mcga.gov.uk/c4mca/mgn_280.pdf**)
>
> 1x multi purpose extinguisher with minimum fire rating 13A 113B or smaller extinguishers with this combined rating. 3x multi purpose extinguishers each with fire rating 5A 34B.

It was not established whether there is an aperture in the engine casing to introduce fire extinguishant into the engine space and this should be verified.

28. LIFESAVING AND EMERGENCY EQUIPMENT

a)   Large quantity of various flares aboard, the majority still in date.
b)   Horseshoe lifebuoy and light in serviceable condition.
c)   Viking 6 man Life raft in a canister, serial no: EO10397, next service due 02/10.

The RNLI operate an excellent free inspection and advice service concerning levels of safety equipment (SEA Check) and can be contacted on 08003280600 or via the RNLI website, www.rnli.org.uk. The RYA also publishes a booklet, C8, "The Boat Safety Handbook, and it is suggested this vessel be equipped to the level appropriate to proposed use. Booklet is obtainable from nautical bookshops or direct from the RYA, telephone 01703-627400 or www.rya.org.uk

29. ENGINE AND INSTALLATION

General access is good. 480 hours recorded at control panel
a)   Beds: Of GRP moulded type. No deterioration or movement noted.
b)   Mountings: Of flexible type, crowbar tested and all intact. The metal parts are rusting but sound.
c)   Engine: The Perkins Prima 4 cylinder diesel engine is believed to be model 50 and is not a 4.108 as described in Broker's details. The exterior would benefit from some cleaning and painting where the paint coatings have failed but the engine is reasonably clean with no obvious leak or serious corrosion noted. Cooling is via indirect closed circuit heat exchanger system and the coolant within the header tank was found clean and free from visible oil contamination.

Fig 148

Oil on dipstick clean and free from emulsification. The engine was briefly run and it started instantly from cold once the heater plugs had been operated. It was not run up to working temperature or put under load but for the brief test ran smoothly with no excess smoke. Once running the engine pumped water correctly. Ahead and astern gears were briefly engaged and operated correctly.
d)   Controls: Of single lever cable operated type and in working order.
e)   The engine space is lined with sound deadening material, this intact. It was not established whether it is of the latest fire resistant type.
f)   Exhaust: Of flexible type and in good condition where accessible. A waterlock is fitted to prevent water siphoning back into engine. A gooseneck is fitted to prevent following seas entering system.
g)   The casing of the Hurth mechanical gearbox is a little corroded, this is believed to be due to a leak at the raw water pump or manifold above the gearbox. (Fig 148)

30. FUEL SYSTEM

The stainless steel fuel tank is securely mounted under the port saloon berth and in good condition where accessible. Delivery tubing is copper and flexible fuel hose conforming to ISO 7840 within the engine space. A high specification Racnor combined filter/separator is fitted between tank and lift pump, this easily accessible. It has an audible/visual alarm at the chart table to warn of the presence of water in the fuel. A dipstick is provided. System conforms to the general standards prevailing when vessel was built. No specific hazards were identified and considered fit for use.

31. ACCOMMODATION GENERAL

The accommodation is fitted out to a high standard and the layout is as per the standard design. It remains in good condition and is well set up for serious offshore use with leecloths etc and all sole boards screwed down.

32. GAS INSTALLATION

This boat is not in commercial use so is not required to comply with the MCA Code of Practice, which requires specific standards for gas systems.

The Recreational Craft Directive also contains a mandatory standard for the gas system but this boat pre-dates the RCD and as such the gas system was not installed to a specific standard and is not required to conform to any current standard now.

Irrespective of the above ALL gas systems are subject to the checks listed below as part of this survey. Recommendations will be made where there is an obvious serious safety issue and these must be carried out before use. Suggestions will also be made where appropriate to enhance safety criteria, particularly with systems where there is no mandatory requirement to conform to a standard. It must be understood however that some Insurance companies require a declaration from the assured that the gas system conforms to current standards.

Sources of further information:
www.calormarineshop.co.uk/rules-regs-answer.htm Comprehensive information on standards and best practice.
www.boatsafetyscheme.com Even if your boat is not required to comply with this standard it contains much sensible advice and the manual can be downloaded.

ITEM	RESULT	ACTION REQUIRED (R) Recommendation to be carried out before use. (S) Suggestion only.
Condition and efficiency of self draining bottle storage	Satisfactory	
Age and condition of flexible hose	Hose at gas bottle was manufactured in 02/02. Best practice is to replace hose every 5 years. Unable to eatblish age of armoured hose at cooker but believed to be more recent	Replace hose at gas bottle with new conforming to BS3212 (S)

ITEM	RESULT	ACTION REQUIRED (R) Recommendation to be carried out before use. (S) Suggestion only.
Age and condition of regulator	Satisfactory but unable to establish age.	In view of low cost fit new. (S)
Condition of copper tubing where accessible	Satisfactory	
Is tubing adequately supported and not under stress where accessible?	Satisfactory	
Are all appliances fitted with flame failure devices on all burners, and did these work properly under test?	Nelson cooker is the only apliance. All burners have flame failure and all worked on test.	
Are any appliances requiring flues properly fitted with same?	Not applicable	
Is a gas alarm fitted?	No	Consider fitting gas alarm (S)
Is each appliance fitted with an isolating tap?	Yes	
If fitted did leak bubble tester function?	Not applicable	Consider fitting bubble tester in order to provide convenient regular leak testing (S)

Additional Observations:

The cooker was briefly operated and no obvious leaks were evident.

Please note however this survey is not any kind of gas safety certificate, that is only obtainable in the UK after comprehensive pressure testing and assessment by a qualified person listed on the Gas safe register (formally CORGI) **www.gassaferegister.co.uk**

33. FRESH WATER TANKS AND DELIVERY

Stainless steel tank securely mounted under the stb saloon berth. This has an isolating valve at its aft end, currently seized. Water is delivered to the galley and heads sinks via a pressure pump, this tested and in working order. All pipework in satisfactory condition where accessible. There is a further stainless steel tank on the port side of the walkthrough to aft cabin, this believed to be associated with the watermaker unit mounted here. A valve was noted under the saloon sole just forward of the table and it is believed this controls the transfer pipe between the two tanks.

There is a small leak at the joints in the pipework supplying the galley sink adjacent to the calorifier. The calorifier is mounted in the engine room heated by the engine closed freshwater circuit. Also has a 230v immersion heater type element. All pipework satisfactory and no leaks were noted. Both shower discharge pumps in working order.

34. HEADS

Both manually operated Lavac type heads units in satisfactory condition with no evidence of leaks at the various joints. The aft heads has a stainless steel holding tank fitted under aft berth, tank manufactured in 2000. Diverter valves etc are in working order.

The forward heads unit has a plastic holding tank fitted under the forward berths and this is creating an unpleasant odour. The diverter valves etc are in working order.

35. ELECTRICAL INSTALLATION

12v DC
The batteries are located under the saloon sole at base of companionway, and well secured in place
Two very large batteries are installed, plus a smaller one of about 100ah capacity, this believed to be the dedicated engine starter battery. The large units showed 12.4v on test whilst the smaller one 14v, this being charged by the shorepower supply at time of survey. (Voltage measured with no load applied). A double fuse box of small capacity was noted in the battery space, these fuses corroded.
Master switches are located under a small lifting trap to port of companionway steps.

As far as could be ascertained all circuits are protected by circuit breakers or in line fuses.
All circuits tested and found working apart from the reading light at forward end of saloon port side.
A recent Sterling 4 stage switch mode automatic battery charger/monitor is located in the engine room.
The engine is fitted with a Sterling power uprated alternator and smart regulator to optimise output.

230v AC:
The 230v Shorepower feed has a type approved RCD device fitted, plus dedicated circuit breakers or fuses for the ringmain, immersion heater and battery charger. All the domestic 230v sockets in the vessel showed live/neutral reverse on test and will thus be live when their switches are turned off. It was not possible to verify whether this is due to the supply coming into the vessel or the ships own wiring. This system should not be used till it has been checked by a qualified 230v AC electrician.

36. ELECTRONIC AND NAVIGATION EQUIPMENT

The equipment is as per the Broker's inventory and was tested as far as possible with yacht ashore.
It was noted that an ICOM automatic antennae tuner is mounted in the lazerette.

37. HEATING AND REFRIGERATION

Heating:
An Eberspacher D4 diesel fired heater is installed in the lazerette. The unit is properly installed and the exhaust well lagged. All ducting intact where accessible. The heater did not start on test but this is often the case if it has not been used for some time.

Refrigeration:
The electrically operated Frigomatic unit is mounted under the galley with the cold box adjacent. Unit was started and ran normally for 30 mins.

38.TENDER
An inflatable dinghy was noted in the lazerette but this could not be properly examined.

CONCLUSIONS AND RECOMMENDATIONS

MAINTENANCE OVERVIEW

Cosmetic maintenance: Vessel has had regular cosmetic maintenance carried out to a good standard and is still a very smart vessel.

Technical maintenance: This has been carried out as required including major replacements such as the teak deck and sails".

LIST OF RECOMMENDATIONS

The recommendations made in the report are listed below with their respective page numbers. All recommendations should be carried out before use of vessel.

1. The clips securing on the eyes each end of the steering cables require replacement. It will be necessary to remove all the heavy gear from the lazerette to carry this out and opportunity should be taken to examine the entire assembly as this could not be carried out during the survey (p201).

2. The cutless bearing requires replacement. Whilst this work is being undertaken the wear in the feathering propeller should be checked against Makers tolerances (p202).

3. There is an intake for the salt water pump at the galley teed into the engine cooling water intake and the securing clips on the hose are very corroded. These require replacement and condition of tee piece carefully checking.

The ballvalve for the forward holding tank discharge under forward vee berth requires servicing and the hose clips replaced.

The ill fitting plastic discharge right aft stb side just above the waterline is placing an unfair strain on its flange and is liable to shear. This should be replaced and it is suggested a new fitting of bronze be obtained (p205).

4. The bolts securing the ¾ forestay chainplate to the anchor well bulkhead should be drawn for full inspection (p206).

5. The provision of fire extinguishers is not considered adequate and should be increased.
The following is considered a minimum and is based on the requirement for a vessel of this size and type found in the MCA Code of Practice (**http://mcga.gov.uk/c4mca/mgn_280.pdf**).

1x multi purpose extinguisher with minimum fire rating 13A 113B or smaller extinguishers with this combined rating.

3x multi purpose extinguishers each with fire rating 5A 34B (p209).

CONCLUSIONS

The Example 48 yacht "Anonymous" is in sound structural condition and very good general condition for her age. She has clearly had regular maintenance and upgrading, and the work required as identified by this survey is no more than general maintenance to be expected at this age.

She is a high quality and very strong yacht which will take her Owners anywhere they wish to sail.

VALUATION:

This Valuation forms the last numbered page of the Report and should be removed to preserve confidentially if required.

Subject: Example 48 class yacht, "Anonymous".

In her present condition as surveyed 2/1/10 I estimate the above vessel to have a Current Market Value in the region of £158000, (one hundred and fifty eight thousand pounds).

The valuation assumes the engine to be in good running order when put under full load which was not possible during this survey.

The foregoing is a standard survey of a well known design generally in good condition. The survey extracts elsewhere give an indication as to how various other more serious defects are expressed in reports.

If you have got this far you may be serious about joining us lucky folk who work in this fascinating field. The practical course at **www.ibtc.co.uk**, where you will see hundreds of defects on real boats, could be your next move.

Good luck!

INDEX

Printed in the USA
CPSIA information can be obtained
at www.ICGtesting.com
LVHW082001220124
769617LV00002B/12

9 781408 114032